Professionalism and Leadership i Childhood Education and Care

Professionalism and Leadership in Early Childhood Education and Care explores the tension between what early years practitioners are expected to achieve, and the level of expertise and understanding required to underpin this. It examines the impact of recent policies on the agency of individual practitioners, and the culture and ethos of their settings, and questions the driving factors behind reforms to curriculum and practice and where this locates practitioners and their provision.

Bringing together the latest research and ideas on professionalism and leadership, the book explores how professional status is understood and acquired and what makes this problematic in ECEC. It explores the impact of different leadership approaches, what needs to be challenged and sets out how the workforce might assert its own identity and values and continue to advocate for the needs of young children.

Including case studies to illustrate the lived experiences of individual practitioners as they worked towards becoming graduate professionals, this will be valuable reading for early years professionals engaged in undergraduate and postgraduate study and those researching policy development and professional identity within ECEC.

Mary A. Dyer is Subject Leader for the Undergraduate Framework courses in the School of Education and Professional Development at the University of Huddersfield, teaching undergraduate and postgraduate courses in Early Childhood Studies. Research interests include ethical practice in early years, professional identity and critical reflection.

Samantha McMahon is Senior Lecturer and Director of Student Retention at the University of Huddersfield, teaching undergraduate and postgraduate courses in Early Childhood Studies. Research interests include professionalism and leadership in ECEC.

Professionalism and Leadership in Early Childhood Education and Care

Mary A. Dyer and Samantha McMahon

Routledge
Taylor & Francis Group

LONDON AND NEW YORK

Cover image: © Getty Images

First published 2023
by Routledge
4 Park Square, Milton Park, Abingdon, Oxon OX14 4RN

and by Routledge
605 Third Avenue, New York, NY 10158

Routledge is an imprint of the Taylor & Francis Group, an informa business

British Library Cataloguing-in-Publication Data
A catalogue record for this book is available from the British Library

Library of Congress Cataloging-in-Publication Data
Names: Dyer, Mary A., 1962- author. | McMahon, Samantha, 1963- author.
Title: Professionalism and leadership in early childhood education and care / Mary A. Dyer, Samantha McMahon.
Description: First Edition. | New York : Routledge, 2023.
| Includes bibliographical references and index. | Identifiers: LCCN 2022025839
| ISBN 9780367415914 (Hardback) | ISBN 9780367415921 (Paperback)
| ISBN 9780367815387 (eBook)
Subjects: LCSH: Early childhood education--Great Britain. | Teaching--Vocational guidance--Great Britain. | Professional socialization--Great Britain
| Early childhood teachers--Professional ethics--Great Britain | Early childhood teachers--Training of--Great Britain. | Child care workers--Training of--Great Britain. | Early childhood education--Study and teaching--Great Britain.
Classification: LCC LB1139.3.G7 D94 2023 |
DDC 372.210941--dc23/eng/20220701
LC record available at https://lccn.loc.gov/2022025839

ISBN: 978-0-367-41591-4 (hbk)
ISBN: 978-0-367-41592-1 (pbk)
ISBN: 978-0-367-81538-7 (ebk)

DOI: 10.4324/9780367815387

Typeset in Sabon
by SPi Technologies India Pvt Ltd (Straive)

Contents

Introduction

As academics working to further the professional education of the early years workforce, we have long been struck, not only by the expertise of practitioners and the personal investment they bring to their practice, but also by how low their expectations can be for any recognition from their service users, employers or regulators. Government funding at the start of the 21st century, intended to raise qualifications and to extend the size and scope of the early years sector, along with Sure Start initiatives to secure all-round, multi-agency family support, should have raised the profile of the early years practitioner as an advocate and support for the children and families they worked with. Yet the phrase 'I'm just a nursery nurse' remains a familiar one to anyone delivering the Level 3 qualifications essential for them to lead educational provision and care for young children. It raises the question of how a workforce can fulfil a role regarded as central to young children's well-being and educational outcomes, yet still be regarded as lesser, by themselves and often the other agencies they work alongside. The aim of this book is to demonstrate how the current policy context in England for ECEC (Early Childhood Education and Care) practice and provision has limited the agency and status of these practitioners through workforce reforms and a professionalisation agenda which, although offering degree-level professional education, has not led to any higher status or regard for practitioners.

Uniquely, this book draws on data collected as part of the authors' doctoral research, to give voice to the workforce themselves and to bring to life their experiences of working in such a complex field. Chapters 1–7 each explore a different aspect of the early years sector and how these impact its workforce, while the final chapter returns to the voices of the workforce.

Chapter 1: 'The English early years sector'. In this chapter we explore the development of the ECEC sector in England and a range of factors which shape the role, status and identity of the ECEC practitioner. The perpetuating vocational habitus of practitioners is explained and how this, alongside contradictions in policy and constructions of the workforce and sector, continues to undermine professional status.

Chapter 2: 'Professionalisation and the early years workforce' examines the policy landscape which has been significant in driving workforce reform in ECEC in England and internationally, and discusses how the disparities between education and care impede professionalisation and what significant stakeholders can do to move it forward.

Chapter 3: 'Constructing a professional identity, claiming professional agency' draws on a range of theoretical frameworks to explore how professional identity is constructed, individually and socially. It includes data and findings from Mary Dyer's doctoral work to argue that professionalisation can only be achieved through an investment in human capital, and if the workforce acquires decisional capital whereby they use their judgement and agency to decide on good and appropriate practice.

Chapter 4: 'Leadership and professionalisation' provides insight into a range of prevailing models of leadership found in the sector and then proposes a new model, the Change Curve Four Frame Model of Leadership, based on findings from Samantha McMahon's doctoral research. The model reflects the unique features of ECEC, for example, the gendered workforce, organisational culture and the challenge of leading change through influence rather than authority.

Chapter 5: 'Reconceptualising professionalism in ECEC' considers new models of professionalism in England and internationally, and the connection between these models and leadership is explored. The chapter argues that a new model of professionalism is emerging which aligns with democratic and relational models of leadership and reflects what matters to practitioners, an ethic of care and professional love.

Chapter 6: 'Practice standards and the shaping of professional identity: Technicians or creative researchers?' This chapter charts, examines and compares professional standards and competencies in ECEC and discusses how these align with conceptualisations of professionalism and what the graduate practitioner has identified as important. The chapter argues that these externally imposed standards, along with practice guidance and the current terms and conditions of service, limit decisional capital of the practitioner and professionalism of the workforce.

Chapter 7: 'Unpicking the role of reflection and a transformative pedagogy for professional education'. This chapter discusses the constraints on professional recognition and identity exercised by a narrow vocational habitus, the regulatory frameworks determining pedagogy, and practice and workforce reform which focus on individual human capital. The chapter argues that transformative approaches to education emphasising critical reflection would support practitioners to acquire decisional capital and agency to challenge and re-define their position, role and professional identity.

Chapter 8: 'Empowerment and agency: Reflections on narratives of practice'. This final chapter draws extensively on data from the authors' doctoral research to illustrate the lived experiences of individual practitioners as they worked towards becoming graduate professionals. Within the participants' narratives are stories of transformation for the individual, their pedagogy and practice and also the weary acknowledgement that professionalisation from above has not brought increased recognition and status to the sector. Therefore, the chapter argues for a career infrastructure that recognises and values the graduate professional leader. However, it also recognises that the workforce must take ownership of their knowledge base and work collectively extending their community of practice beyond the individual setting. HEIs and other stakeholders must support and legitimise their collective endeavour, but ultimately ECEC professionalism must come from within the sector.

This book brings together, in one place, current research and ideas on professionalism and leadership, in England and internationally. Its intended readership includes early years professional educators/teachers engaged in undergraduate and postgraduate study and research into policy development within the ECEC sector, leadership and professional identity. For the workforce, this book is further intended to extend a critical understanding of professionalism and leadership in ECEC, support professional development and contribute to research in the field so that practitioners will build, and own, their professional knowledge. We hope that the book will inspire students and practitioners to become leaders who look beyond their setting, to work together to develop a collective professional identity which advocates for greater professional recognition, and that educators will support this through a transformative model of professional education.

Glossary

CWDC	Children's Workforce Development Council
DES	Department of Education and Science
DfE	Department for Education
DfEE	Department for Education and Employment
DfES	Department for Education and Skills
DH	Department of Health
ECEC	Early Childhood Education and Care
ECGP	Early Childhood Graduate Practitioner
ECGPC	Early Childhood Graduate Practitioner Competencies
ECM	Every Child Matters
EPPE	Effective Provision of Pre-School Education
EYE	Early Years Educator
EYFS	Early Years Foundation Stage
EYP	Early Years Professional
EYP	Early Years Professional Status
YET	Early Years Teacher
EYTS	Early Years Teacher Status
GCSE	General Certificate in Secondary Education
HMSO	Her Majesty's Stationary Office
LA	Local Authority
NCTL	National College for Teaching and Leadership
NDNA	National Day Nurseries Association
NNEB	National Nursery Examination Board
NVQ	National Vocational Qualification
OECD	Organisation for Economic Cooperation and Development
Ofsted	Office for Standards in Education
ONS	Office for National Statistics
PVI	Private Voluntary and Independent
QCA	Qualifications Curriculum Authority
QTS	Qualified Teacher Status
SSLP	Sure Start Local Programme
TA	Teaching Agency

Chapter 1

The English early years sector

Introduction

This chapter describes the structure of the sector, identifying it as largely private provision that is subject to government regulation, and considers what this means for the roles and responsibilities of the workforce. It identifies some of the contradictions and paradoxes, as well as changing discourses associated with the early years sector and how these have shaped the role, status and identity of the early years practitioner. It identifies key stakeholders who have influenced the role of the practitioner and the discourse of practice, and explores how these, along with societal expectations and initial training, have contributed to a vocational habitus for practitioners that continues to undermine a claim to professional status. It considers how a neoliberal approach from government to the regulation and long-term sustainability of provision has impacted the identity of early years practitioners and currently works to put private provision at risk. It concludes by identifying the significant power relationships between the sector and its stakeholders, and how these have shaped its structure and the development of its workforce.

Some facts and figures

The early years sector in England today is a mix of government-controlled and government-funded provision, privately owned and managed businesses, and voluntary, community-run provision and social service, with over 80% of provision situated within PVI (private, voluntary and independent) provision (DfE, 2019, p. 4) (Table 1.1).

In addition to this, Reception class provision based in primary schools is still regulated by the EYFS, whilst also introducing children to the more formal practice and pedagogy of the National Curriculum and Key Stage 1. This distribution of provision means there is considerable variation across the workforce in terms of job roles and descriptions, and terms of employment and levels of remuneration. The only common condition of employment across the sector is the Early Years Foundation Stage (EYFS) Statutory Requirements (DfE, 2021). Most practitioners are working in settings that meet the minimum requirement that 50% of the staff should be qualified to Level 2, staff in senior roles to Level 3 (DfE, 2021), and where there is no mandatory requirement for higher levels of qualification within staff teams.

The size of the sector has remained relatively stable in recent years, with 72,100 settings in 2016, and rising to 73,100 in 2018, and the PVI settings accounting for over 80% of provision. However, there are now concerns over sustainability of provision,

DOI: 10.4324/9780367815387-1

Table 1.1 Early years provision in England, 2019

	No. of settings	% of sector	No. of places	% of sector
PVI – group-based provision	24,000	33%	1,088,100	66%
Child-minder provision	39,400	55%	239,700	14%
School-based provision	9,100	12.5%	330,300	20%
	72,500		1,655,800	

(Data drawn from DfE, 2019)

as economic pressures arising from recent COVID-19 lockdown measures and stagnating funding for nursery education places threaten the viability of provision offered by PVI organisations. This puts the future employment prospects at risk for around 85% of the workforce, at a time when government rhetoric continues to emphasise the economic need for parents to be in paid employment, and the educational necessity for children to take up their funded nursery entitlement in order to benefit fully from school.

State influence on the early years sector

The development of the sector has most recently been driven through government-sponsored growth of private provision (see Table 1.2), with an increased focus on its capacity to support working parents and improve children's educational outcomes. At the same time, the discourse of practice, those systems that define the sector and its purpose in relation to government agenda (Osgood, 2006, p. 8), has changed, driven by state intervention, and fluctuating government priorities for young children – from addressing child poverty and damaging home environments, to improving multi-agency safeguarding practice, to raising educational outcomes and promoting school readiness.

The expansion of state-funded nursery education and family support provision since the start of the 21st century has positioned the sector as 'almost as cure for all social and economic ills' (Cohen et al., 2004, p. 57) including:

- issues of poverty and deprivation and their impact on children's well-being, health and potential for future employment
- the need for an educated, available workforce, to ensure economic stability and reduce welfare spending
- addressing safeguarding issues
- the recurring issue of young children's school readiness, and the affordability of provision to support this
- the outcomes of poor parenting on children's educability and future employment.

(adapted from Cohen et al., 2004, p. 57)

Consequently, the early years sector has become a more diverse and multipurpose service with responsibility for fulfilling a broad social and governmental agenda. The current

Table 1.2 Government policy initiatives to expand and support early years provision in England

The National Childcare Strategy: meeting the childcare challenge (DfEE, 1998)	• Expansion of the PVI sector through Neighbourhood Nursery Initiative (NNI) funding; funding of Out of School Club (OOSC) provision; introduction of local authority Early Years Development and Childcare Partnerships (EYDCPs) to support local providers; proposals for SSLPs and Extended schools • Workforce development funding to raise number of Level 2 and Level 3 qualified staff • Introduction of Nursery Expansion Grant (NEG), enabling more PVI settings to offer nursery education, and Nursery Education Funding (NEF) to pay for nursery education for three- and four-year-olds for 12.5 hours per week
Sure Start Local Programme (SSLP) initiative (Bate and Foster, 2017) Expansion of SSLP to Sure Start Children's Centres (DfES, 2004a; DfES, 2007; DfE, 2013)	• Funding to tackle the impact of poverty and disadvantage on young children in areas of greatest deprivation; later rolled out as Children's Centres that offered heath, education and financial advice for families, with the intention of there being one in every ward within a local authority
Curriculum Guidance for the Foundation Stage (QCA/DfEE, 2000) Every Child Matters (ECM) (DfES, 2004b) Children Act 2004 Childcare Act, 2006	• Curriculum support for providers of nursery education, including PVI settings • Definition of positive outcomes for children • New legislation enacting the principles of ECM, making it the duty of local authorities to ensure effective multi-agency working is in place
2005 Introduction of Children's Workforce Development Council (CWDC) Workforce Reform Strategy (DfES, 2006)	• CWDC introduced to oversee workforce reforms, including meeting the target for all settings to have graduate leadership, and to develop the criteria for this as Early Years Professional Status (EYPS) • Transformation Fund to offer support for employers (and individuals) to meet targets for more highly qualified staff • Introduction of Common Core of Skills and Knowledge (CWDC, 2010) for all practitioners working with children and young people
Review of early years qualifications (Nutbrown, 2012) Early Years Workforce Strategy (DfE, 2017)	• Review of early years qualifications and role of practitioner • Revision of English and Maths qualifications for Early Years Educators

focus, which rests on children's educational outcomes and their preparation for formal schooling, can be seen in a growing assessment agenda and curriculum framework reform, as well as an increased emphasis on the number of children being judged to achieve a 'good level of development' (DfE, 2020, p. 6) by the end of their nursery education.

The policy and legislation changes introduced to develop and regulate the sector's capacity and purpose demonstrate the increasing power of the state to shape the discourse of practice and the role of the practitioner, whilst apparently remaining at the periphery of what is largely a privately owned and managed sector. The overarching discourse of provision and practice, it could be argued, has shifted from promoting the needs and rights of the child, to a deficit construction of the child as being at risk, or in need of education, and to prioritising the needs of the working parent through presenting early years provision as a commoditised service. The introduction of national assessment measures to ensure an effective engagement with compulsory, formal education has further shaped the purpose of early years practice as responsible for ensuring children's school readiness. Children are now understood not only as vulnerable to the actions of adults and therefore in need of monitoring and surveillance, but also as entitled to a series of guaranteed outcomes in life, and preparation for school and formal education. Early years provision is therefore not only a developmental benefit for young children and of practical value to the working parent, but also a political tool to be used in developing and safeguarding the workforce of the future. It might then be anticipated that the status and role of the practitioner should also develop and grow, reflecting their increased responsibilities.

The workforce has similarly been defined and shaped by these changes, being transformed from well-intentioned, morally fit carers and substitute parents, into competent educators with a multidisciplinary role, and encouraged to operate as entrepreneurs, competing in a neoliberal market for early years provision. However, the early years practitioner, who began in private practice as a highly qualified expert with a specific, critical understanding of young children's developmental needs, is now characterised as a competent technician (Moss, 2006) who ensures children's development is appropriately promoted, and their learning appropriately supervised and measured, through the use of regulatory frameworks and generic good practice guides. Demands on early years provision have expanded but the position and capital of the early years practitioner, it could be argued, have not kept pace. This is due in part to how practitioners present themselves and how their service users habitually perceive them, but also due to levels of pay and funding within the sector, and an infrastructure that only sets out minimal levels of qualification, with no graduate mandate and no nationally recognised job roles and titles.

Problematising the practitioner: Their role, their status, their identity

There is little in education policy that defines the role of the practitioner, or their professional identity, although the context and content of their work offer more insight how they are understood. Bourdieu's concept of habitus, 'systems of durable, transposable dispositions, structured structures, predisposed to function as structuring structures' (Bourdieu, 1977, p. 72), can be used to explain the behaviour of individuals and groups, and the limitations and restrictions they interact within. For early years practitioners these systems include their initial vocational education and its content and pedagogy, the values and attitudes considered appropriate for those caring for young children, and the social approval their role attracts. The agents shaping this habitus therefore include regulators, funders, employers and service users, as well as those designing and delivering professional education to the workforce.

Colley et al. (2003) further identified *vocational* habitus, 'a set of dispositions derived from idealised and realised identities and informed by the notions and guiding ideologies of the vocational culture' (Colley et al., 2003, p. 493). For early years practitioners, this vocational habitus is to be caring and maternal, a description later confirmed by the work of Osgood (2006, 2009, 2010), who described a hyperfeminised workforce, constructed as caring compassionate, nurturing and service-oriented. Earlier work by Skeggs (1988) demonstrated how for young women with few academic qualifications, and who self-identify as not being academically able, the practitioner role is framed as being about doing and feeling, behaving in the right ways and a sense of personal commitment, rather than knowing. Working in early years is presented as a means of achieving moral and social respectability through emotional labour, although this comes at the cost of economic reward. Even today's more highly qualified practitioners appear to accept that the main value of their work comes from approval for their personal commitment rather than financial reward. As one practitioner working in a Children's Centre and about to complete her BA Hons degree put it:

> Childcare – you have to be passionate about doing it as well. Most don't do it for the money, do they?
>
> (Tina)

More recent debate about requiring early years educators to have GCSE grade 4 and above for Maths and English raised concerns over who this might therefore discourage or exclude from the qualified workforce. This perpetuates the privileging of disposition over intellect, almost implying that academic ability and the ability to care form a mutually exclusive binary, and serves to maintain the limited social and cultural capital of the early years practitioner.

The lack of power arising from restricted social and cultural capital arguably underpins acceptance by the early years workforce that this social approval for their work outweighs concerns over status or terms and conditions of employment (Colley, 2006). With the advent of graduate practitioners, following more than a decade of workforce reform strategy, acceptance of exploitation that perpetuates social inequality across the sector should by now be challenged. However, the continuing low rates of pay and qualification observed in the sector today (NDNA, 2019) suggest that for a while at least, the offer of a morally worthwhile occupation remains attractive to potential applicants, including those who consider themselves unqualified for alternative forms of employment. McGillivray (2008) has argued that the role of the practitioner should evolve to combine appropriate disposition with specialist knowledge and career prospects. However, the regulatory framework of the sector continues to provide little infrastructure to support this, despite a range of workforce reform initiatives and targets having been set and revised over the last three decades (Nutbrown, 2012). The high rates of attrition in the PVI settings (NDNA, 2019) would suggest that the attraction of social approval today is short-lived in the context of austerity and rising living costs, and that moral worthiness is not always sufficient compensation for limited career prospects and low pay. However, rather than remain in the early years sector and drive change to terms and conditions of employment, those who are dissatisfied leave, reinforcing their lack of power to effect change either to the infrastructure of the sector or its perceived vocational habitus.

For many practitioners, and for those who fund or use their services, care is seen as central to their role, but this too is problematic. There is a well-established research base that argues that care is essential to supporting the learning and development of young children (Ang, 2014; Davis and Degotardi, 2015). Yet focusing on care as the central discourse of practice emphasises a gendered and interpersonal understanding of the workforce (Moss, 2006), focusing on their disposition and moral fitness for employment, rather than understanding them as professionals who critically apply theoretical knowledge to their practice. This encourages practitioners themselves to understand their role as practical rather than intellectual (Skeggs, 1988; Sims Schouten and Strittrich-Lyons, 2013), devaluing their sense of professional status and reducing their claim to cultural or social capital. This further encourages an essentially technical/rational perception of their role (Schon, 1983), supported by a competence-based approach to their vocational training, and the framing of practice within regulatory requirements and guidance.

In recent years, there has been an increasingly educational emphasis on the content of early years practice, with the reframing and revising of the Early Learning Goals (DfE, 2021) and the introduction of new testing as children enter formal education. An assessment regime designed to measure children's developing literacy and numeracy skills, and to give a starting point for measuring school effectiveness, and Ofsted's characterisation of the EYFS as a vehicle for servicing entry to Key Stage 1 (Ofsted, 2017), appears to privilege measurable educational outcomes rather than holistic development. Current rhetoric about the impact of pandemic lockdown measures leaving even very young children needing to 'catch up' on their education implies a responsibility for practitioners to focus their role on preparing children for the assessment agenda of Reception class and the more formal pedagogy of KS1. Practitioners can therefore now lay claim to more educationally focused job titles (DfE, 2013; Dyer, 2018a, 2018b).

However, this gives rise to a paradox over the role and value of the practitioner. Whilst a school readiness discourse might emphasise the practitioner role in supporting and facilitating early education, this practice remains located within externally set quality frameworks, reliant on staff with relatively low levels of qualification. A focus on the educational and psychological aspects of early years practice might acknowledge the need for a higher level of academic, critical education and training, and a clearer, national career structure, along with commensurate terms and conditions of employment. This, in turn, might more accurately reflect the level of skill and responsibility associated with the task of ensuring children's educational outcomes and psychological development and well-being. It raises the question, however, of why these are not in place, and why nursery education is not better funded.

It could be argued that it is both the nature of early years practice and the regulatory framework for the sector that contribute to a contested definition of the practitioner role. Katz (1985) argued that this is in part due to perceptions of the role of play as a vehicle for learning for young children, rather than simply as a state of being. Her eight criteria for defining the professional status of an occupational group also demonstrate how the current structure of the sector contributes to perpetuating its low status in relation to formal education. Whilst early years practitioners can safely lay claim to providing a service that is altruistic, ethical and socially necessary, its knowledge base is broad and multidisciplinary rather than more narrowly and uniquely defined. Initial training for employment even at senior levels is relatively brief; practice standards are set and regulated by an external authority; and practice outcomes are held accountable to external funders and policymakers; such factors serve to undermine the professional autonomy of the workforce. The centrality of care to the practitioner role, through the development of close, supportive relationships with children and their families, is often foregrounded in the way practitioners describe their role:

We're doing everything we can to make it [the nursery] a home from home environment, just to make sure the parents are as happy as the child really.

(Janet)

The aims of Children's Centres [are] to target families and the only way to target families is to understand families which is to build rapport with families.

(Laura)

However, this means that professional detachment, or objectivity, remains a difficult, or even inappropriate, condition to fulfil. Equally evident in how they describe themselves is their awareness of external pressures and expectations:

[my role is] to follow government guidelines, school policies, early years curriculum, adhere to anything routine, be a key worker, do assessments, observations ... work with parent partnerships.

(Florence)

When this lack of autonomy and ownership of practice is combined with the lack of social and cultural capital of practitioners, it creates a professional identity that is constructed largely in terms of personal commitment and compliance, evidenced through discussions of professionalism based on personal values and interpersonal relationships with children and with colleagues:

I want to improve her [a specific child] development and support her development the best I can.

(Laura)

For me personally ... [I'm] there to work with and support all the rest of the staff team ... it's not just working as the Manager overseeing them, it's working alongside then as well.

(Zoe)

The perpetuating vocational habitus of the early years practitioner, however, is also due to the way in which state intervention has both shaped the operation of the sector, and held back from controlling its structure, through the introduction of new stakeholder groups for early years provision. By taking the neoliberal approach of encouraging private enterprise and allowing market forces to drive the size and shape of the sector, whilst retaining the power to licence provision, successive governments have been able to use early years provision to meet various agenda without incurring the cost of owning and managing provision. Private ownership and autonomous management of provision are effective justification for a seemingly light-touch infrastructure regarding terms and conditions of employment, levels of qualification (to meet minimum regulatory requirements) or career progression across the sector. Government acknowledges its role in overseeing the quality of provision but renders individual entrepreneurs accountable for the sustainability of their provision, through meeting the quality standards of regulators and the service demands of working parents. This approach has enabled successive governments to launch workforce reform agendas that emphasise the professional expertise, autonomy and judgement of practitioners and providers, yet hold back from mandating higher levels of qualifications or introducing a national infrastructure to support this. At the same time, government-led inspection regimes and assessment agenda serve as powerful forces for directing and guiding the operation of private provision.

Emerging stakeholders in early years provision

Children and their learning and developmental needs, it could be argued, were the initial stakeholders in early years provision. The McMillan sisters pioneered charitable work to address deprived children's holistic developmental needs and support parents. The Nursery School Movement of the early 20th century campaigned for school-based provision to address the needs of very young children requiring safe supervision and opportunities for learning before the age of 5, whose families were unable to offer this at home. Isaacs (1929) argued that formal education provision for older children was not an appropriate care and developmental approach for very young children below the age of 5, introducing a discourse of play-based practice to support the holistic development of the individual child, and to ensure children experienced a healthy and emotionally secure childhood. Psychologists, educational specialists and philanthropists recognised the need for young children to be offered opportunities and resources to support their development and learning. Early leaders of practice argued that sensitivity, affection and responsiveness on the part of the knowledgeable practitioner were essential for effective early years practice (Isaacs, 1929; Aslanian, 2015), along with a holistic, less formal approach to supporting the learning of very young children (Owen, 1920).

The emergence of government social policy agenda and the needs of working parents as major stakeholders in early years provision can be argued to underpin changes to the discourse of early years practice. The establishment of the State as a key stakeholder in the early years sector has always been contingent on how well the sector can support the achievement of government agenda. The initial introduction of nursery education, it was acknowledged by early pioneers (Owen, 1920, p. x), would require new government spending, which would achieve public support only if the provision were seen to be effective. The introduction of workplace nurseries during WWII was essential to support the female workforce required to maintain the economy and the war effort, and the rapid dissolution of the same nurseries was done to ensure employment for the demobilised military veterans (Lea, 2014). Recommendations concerning the value of pre-school provision to support young children's transition to school (DES, 1967) were not implemented for economic reasons until there was sufficient capacity in the private sector to meet demand, and until that provision could be effectively quality assured. Thus, the shape and capacity of the early years sector, and the purpose of its provision, have altered to meet the requirements of this significant stakeholder, which positions government as mediating between a private sector and the needs of individual children and their families to meet broader societal requirements.

Significant state involvement in workforce development for the sector began in 1945, through the sponsoring by the Ministry of Health, of the National Nursery Examination Board (NNEB) to train and qualify practitioners. The formation of the NNEB national qualification created a discourse of practice that emphasised the importance of health and the prevention of disease (Meering, 1947). However, it also established a perception that good practice could be delivered through following guidelines, regulations and set procedures rather than requiring the interpretation of developmental theory and research. The practitioner was characterised as a substitute parent and compliant guardian of the child's safety and well-being, rather than an expert in early learning. The introduction of the Children Act (1989) further reinforced this discourse centring on the child and his/her welfare, and established the role of the State in overseeing the quality of practice. Local authorities were now required to register and inspect early years provision, and the legal provisions of the Act reinforced a discourse of care and child protection arising from children's perceived vulnerability in early years settings and the family home. Whilst emphasising the role of the practitioner as the protector of the vulnerable, again they were deemed to need a clear, legal framework to guide them in broader, safeguarding responsibilities. Underpinning the 1989 Children Act, therefore, and the registration requirements that followed it, remained the concept that following set processes and procedures could achieve good practice.

State-funded nursery education was first proposed in the early 20th century (Owen, 1920, p. x), but to be effective, and thereby justify government spending, this would necessitate the employment of expert specialists. Following the 1908 Education Act, a small number of state nursery schools were introduced in 1923, adopting a pedagogy and curriculum more appropriate to the learning needs of children aged between three and five, which was delivered by trained teachers, recognising that children's early learning required the support of a qualified practitioner with specialist knowledge. Two later government reports (DES, 1967; Rumbold, 1990) also highlighted the value of pre-school provision in preparing children for formal education. They strongly advocated a play-based approach to young children's learning and the necessity of treating children as individuals, and meeting their unique learning needs. Both identified the need for sensitive and knowledgeable practitioners, regarding interaction with adults as the key to successful learning and development, echoing the calls of the earlier pioneers. Although this might be construed as recognising the child as a stakeholder, by supporting their preparation for school, the fact that cost effectiveness drove the decision not to make nursery education a universal offer until the end of the 20th century indicates the primacy of economic concerns.

The government decision not to implement the recommendations of the Plowden Report (DES, 1967) led to an increase in the formation of community-based, voluntary pre-school provision, through the formation of the Pre-School Playgroups Association (PPA, now Early Alliance). The development of this parent-led, voluntary pre-school provision for young children, it could be argued, is what has contributed to the perception of children's play as a social, rather than an educational, phenomenon, only requiring the support of a well-intentioned and interested adult, which continued to be reflected in the registration requirements set out in the Children Act 1989. This somewhat superficial perception overlooks the arguments of earlier, highly educated early years pioneers that young children's learning is socially constructed, best facilitated through child-led play, and requires a positive and stable emotional environment for the children to thrive. It should also be remembered that the PPA itself challenged the perception that pre-school practice requires only good intentions and a positive disposition towards young children, rather than a research-led knowledge base, by introducing training for its groups and members, leading to qualifications that still have currency in the sector today.

The role of government as a stakeholder in early years provision was further established as guidance for nursery education provision was issued from 1996, alongside the release of government funding for nursery education places in private settings. This outlined the curriculum providers should follow, and the outcomes children should meet (SCAA, 1996; QCA/DfES, 2000) in their nursery education, enabling the measurement and assessment of their progress, and school readiness. This enabled the quality assurance of the private sector, to demonstrate the effective use of public funding, and was instrumental in driving the expansion overall of the early years sector through a mix of state and private providers. Thus, the State was able to protect its interests and promote the development of an independent sector, furthering its social policy agenda, without taking on the cost of ensuring the sustainability of this provision. By locating this oversight as external to individual providers, this further emphasises the perception of early years practitioners as competent, compliant technicians with caring dispositions and answerable to powerful stakeholders, rather than as autonomous, qualified experts in children's holistic learning and development.

There was also recognition early as the 1908 Education Act that many young children from poorer families were living in poor-quality homes in unhealthy environments. Health surveillance and monitoring of these children could be carried out more regularly if they were attending nursery school, and parents would be better educated about the care their children required (Owen, 1920). Once again, the role of government as a powerful stakeholder was established, this time based on a discourse of intervention, aimed at addressing issues of child health and social and economic deprivation, whilst supporting 'all round development of the mind and body in an atmosphere of happy companionship' (Owen, 1920, pp. 12, 13). This same discourse perpetuates today, with the early 21st-century establishment of Sure Start Local Programmes (SSLPs) and Children's Centres (Sure Start, 2005; Bate and Foster, 2017), and significant reports concerning children's outcomes and social mobility (Field, 2010; Allen, 2011). Whilst it could be argued that this has re-established the child as the principle stakeholder and beneficiary of this provision, Children Centre core support included advice to parents on employment and training, and was underpinned initially by the Every Child Matters outcomes (DfES, 2004b). This linkage demonstrates again that government-funded early years provision was being deployed to support a broader social policy and welfare to work agenda, as well as potentially promoting a functionalist perspective on socialising children and their parents into a positive perception of education and employment.

Establishing the State as a key stakeholder in private provision has led to the development of a practitioner role that goes beyond a caring disposition, and a sole concern for the child's learning and development. Children's Centre provision created new roles for early years practitioners, requiring partnership working with parents and other agencies as planned interventions to address children's needs. The discourse of the sector expanded from being one of concern over children's safety and well-being to including support for parents' employment and educational needs in the interests of the wider national economy, and providing family support. The Every Child Matters outcomes are now no longer part of official government policy for children's services, but Children's Centres have retained, even through significant public sector cuts, their focus on the most needy and vulnerable of families, requiring their practitioners to maintain their support role. This has changed the nature of the parent–practitioner relationship, from one solely of customer/retailer or service user/service provider, to one where the practitioner in some settings has some delegated authority to advise parents/carers and even monitor their behaviour. However, there has been no change the vocational training or qualification requirements of the workforce, continuing to position them as subordinate to health, social work and teaching professionals, despite their more constant and immediate relationship with parents/carers and children.

The State itself went on to establish parents as stakeholders through the introduction of the National Childcare Strategy (DfEE, 1998), as the Labour government sought to encourage all parents to seek employment or training, and thereby support themselves and their families. The aim of the Strategy was to ensure accessible, affordable, high-quality childcare for all parents who needed it. Thus the government presented the early years sector as a commoditised service to parents, supplemented by tax credits and voucher schemes, in support of broader economic aims. The size of the early years sector was greatly and rapidly increased by means of funding streams including the Neighbourhood Nurseries Initiative, Nursery Expansion Grant and New Opportunities Funding, to ensure sufficiency and affordability of provision, particularly in deprived areas, where there was deemed to be a pressing need to support parents into employment or training. Nursery education was offered universally, initially to four-year-olds, then extended to three-year-olds, with the pattern of delivery fixed at five daily short sessions across three school terms, to match the delivery pattern of the school year. Current rules for how parents can use this subsidised provision now allow much more flexibility to match the demands of a working day, and the needs of the working parent. Arguably, the focus of early years provision had now shifted to providing a service for working parents rather than a universal, or even remedial, benefit for young children and their development. This continues today with the further extension of nursery education funding, to provide 30 hours of provision specifically to the children of working parents. That it had been done predominantly to enable parents to work and thus reduce welfare spending, rather than to benefit children's learning and development, can be seen in urgency with which additional care places were made available, the changes to the pattern of delivery and in the relatively low level of professional education required for a largely unqualified workforce.

The professional context of the early years practitioner today

Overall, changes to the discourse of early years practice, whilst changing the focus of the purpose of early years provision, still combine to frame the role of the practitioner as competent, caring and compliant with external regulation. Early Years practitioners have acquired additional responsibilities for promoting children's well-being and supporting their health and educational outcomes. Yet there has been little change to mandatory minimum requirements for qualified staff or ongoing training within settings, despite the increased complexities of the practitioner role. Funding for the vital nursery education they provide has remained at its lowest level over the last four years (NDNA, 2019), despite the costs of such provision increasing. The growing complexities of the practitioner role, it could be argued, have left them needing an even greater understanding of children's health, development and educational needs. Despite the call from pioneers of early years practice for highly qualified experts in child development to support the learning and development of very young children, recruitment to the sector has drawn from a gendered, largely unqualified workforce, whose disposition to care and moral fitness to practice has been valued over their intellectual capacities or achievements. Mandatory vocational training now stops at Level 3 for supervisory staff, (DfE, 2021) and child-minders are only required to undergo limited basic training (DfE, 2021). There remains no infrastructure across the sector to encourage higher-level qualifications, and the cost of such education to the individual practitioner means they need to change their job role to make such investment worthwhile. Such framing acts as a boundary to the identity of the early years practitioner, defining not only who they are but also what they are not allowed or expected to be.

The early years sector needs to address a number of questions about its purpose and status. The current combination of political stakeholders and consumers, along with a wide-ranging perception of the purpose of early years provision, has led to a conflation of terms for early years settings (West and Noden, 2016) – *play* groups, pre-*schools*, day *care*, nursery *school* – that sends out a mixed message about the role and expertise of the practitioner. This apparently arbitrary and unnecessary divide between care and education practice (Rumbold, 1990) presents the former as a matter of disposition and fitness (medically, legally, morally) to practice, whilst characterising the latter as requiring academic qualifications, and delivery through following practice guidance whilst subject to quality assurance from external regulators. There is increasing State oversight of the sector as a whole, including the licensing, quality assurance and regulation of provision, with a strong emphasis on educational practice to secure children's learning outcomes. There remains a tension between early years provision (particularly its educational component) presented as a universal, sometimes remedial, benefit for all children, or as a commodity sold to benefit working parents and support a failing economy. Initial workforce reform rhetoric (DfES, 2006) called for a more knowledgeable workforce to ensure better outcomes for children, yet there is still no mandate for highly qualified practitioners, capable of managing, leading and critically reflecting on practice to drive this improvement. The sector itself comprises over 70,000 small organisations, owned and managed by individuals or small chains, so there are no nationally agreed job titles, descriptions or personal specifications for their roles; no nationally agreed levels of responsibility an individual practitioner may be expected to take on and no nationally agreed terms and conditions for their employment beyond legal requirements set out in law for all employers to meet. What might appear to be free market flexibility for the sector is actually confusing to parents and employers (Nutbrown, 2012), and offers no recognised career pathway, progression or security for practitioners.

Finally and ironically, the early years workforce in England is now arguably at risk from the market-driven, neoliberal approach introduced through state-funded expansion, to meet parental demand and fulfil government agenda. Government funding no longer covers the cost of nursery education places, and private and voluntary organisations struggle to maintain the financial viability of their settings. Qualified and experienced practitioners are leaving the sector for better-paid, more highly valued, less stressful or more secure employment (Table 1.3).

Current rates of pay, on average, are no better than government set levels of minimum wage (NDNA, 2019), which offers little financial scope or incentive for pursuing professional development qualifications. Early years settings have to commit over 70% of their income to staff costs and must meet statutory requirements for staffing levels. Competitive pricing and value for money offer limited scope for the higher salaries and larger staff teams that could ease some of the pressure contributing to current high levels of attrition across the workforce. The original government ambition of early years practice being led by a graduate in every setting (DfES, 2006) looks less likely to be achieved in a context where graduate jobs have more than halved, and PVI settings report that they are finding it increasingly difficult to meet the costs of a graduate's

Table 1.3 Early years workforce qualifications – PVI settings (England)

	2015/16	2016/17	2017/18	2018/19
Unqualified and apprenticeship trainees			10%	26%
NVQ Level 2 or equivalent			11	17
NVQ Level 3 or equivalent (EYE)	83	75	66	52
Graduate/YET (previously EYPS)			13	5

(Data drawn from NDNA, 2019)

salary (NDNA, 2019). More worryingly, the clear trend for early years settings now to be operating at the minimal required levels for qualified staff (DfE, 2021) puts pressure on this declining group to oversee the practice and professional education of an increasing number of trainees and assistants. There is a clear tension between portraying the sector as the essential underpinning of children's success in Key Stage 1, even as the 'saviour sibling' of early education and health services, and then stepping back from developing the infrastructure and funding support that is needed to reflect the importance of its role.

Conclusion

What emerges from these tensions and the trajectory of policy development for the sector is an indication of where the power lies to drive its development, and define the role of its workforce. The early years sector today is a network of power relationships between different stakeholders who hold an interest in its successful operation. Each group pursues a different agenda, with different levels of power to support their influence, and arguably with different criteria for measuring success. These stakeholders include:

- politicians and policymakers at government level
- employers and owners seeking to run cost-effective and sustainable businesses (for both profit and not-for profit)
- charitable and voluntary bodies aiming to address issues of inequality, need and deprivation on behalf of children
- parents seeking safe and high-quality care and education for their children
- children themselves requiring support for their successful learning and development
- practitioners seeking a rewarding form of employment, and a career structure within which they can progress.

Arguably the most meaningful relationship, in terms of its balance of power, is the one between government and providers and practitioners, as the former controls the policy and regulation that governs the sector, with which the latter must comply to retain their licence to practice. Spencer-Woodley (2014, p. 33) described this relationship as a 'living contradiction', where accountability to government definitions of standards and quality has a detrimental effect on practitioners' abilities to underpin their practice with their own values, experience and judgement, at a time when their role is becoming more complex and multifaceted. Continuing emphasis on a neoliberal understanding of early years provision presents the sector solely as a commodity purchased to support working parents and to improve children's educational outcomes. This limits the power of the individual practitioner to define their own role and determine their own value within this marketplace, perpetuating instead a vocational habitus and professional identity of compliance and subordination.

How then can practitioners address this habitus and change public and even political perceptions of their role? A national infrastructure that offers a framework for career development and expands the level of qualifications required for more senior roles could support practitioners and providers in challenging a public perception of their work as interpersonally and practically, rather than intellectually, underpinned. A pull back on regulatory oversight in the form of practice guidance and assessment agenda would give space for more child-centred practice and the exercise of an individual's professional values and judgement. It could be argued that a nationally led workforce reform, including access to higher levels of professional education, is what would offer practitioners the opportunity to develop individually as experts and specialists, so that there is a workforce available to exercise this judgement and take on the higher responsibilities now being asked of them. But infrastructure without qualified staff and workforce reform without the opportunity to exercise greater expertise or the incentive of career development are unlikely to be effective. The following chapter considers how workforce reform has been applied in the early years sector to raise the quality of practice and to develop the practitioner role, and the extent of its success in resolving the contradiction of developing autonomy and agency within a powerful regulatory context.

References

Allen, G. (2011). *Early Intervention: The Next Steps*. London: Crown Copyright.

Ang, L. (2014). Pre-school or prep school? Rethinking the role of early years education. *Contemporary Issues in Early Childhood*, 15 (2), 185–199.

Aslanian, T. K. (2015). Getting behind discourses of love, care and maternalism in early childhood education. *Contemporary Issues in Early Years*, 16 (2), 153–165.

Bate, A. and Foster, D. (2017). *Briefing Paper no. 7257: Sure Start (England)*. London: House of Commons Library.

Bourdieu, P. (1977). *Outline of a Theory of Practice*. Cambridge: Cambridge University Press.

Children's Workforce Development Council (CWDC) (2010). *The Common Core of Skills and Knowledge: At the Heart of What You Do*. Leeds: CWDC.

Cohen, B., Moss, P., Petrie, P. and Wallace, J. (2004). *A New Deal for Children? Re-forming Education and Care in England, Scotland and Sweden*. University of Bristol: Policy Press.

Colley, H. (2006). Learning to labour with feeling: Class, gender and emotions in childcare education and training. *Contemporary Issues in Early Childhood*, 7 (1), 15–29.

Colley, H., James, D., Dimont, K. and Tedder, M. (2003). Learning as becoming in vocational education and training: Class, gender and the role of vocational habitus. *Journal of Vocational Education and Training*, 55 (4), 471–498.

Davis, B. and Degotardi, S. (2015). Who cares? Infant educators' responses to professional discourses of care. *Early Child Development and Care*, 185, 11–12, 1733–1747.

Department for Education (DfE) (2013). *More Great Childcare: Raising Quality and Giving Parents More Choice.* Crown Copyright. Department for Education - (publishing.service.gov.uk)

Department for Education and Employment (DfEE) (1998). *The National Childcare Strategy: Meeting the Childcare Challenge.* London: HMSO.

Department for Education and Science (DES) (1967). *The Plowden Report: Children and Their Primary Schools.* London: HMSO.

DfE (2017). *Early Years Workforce Strategy.* London: DfE.

DfE (2019). *Survey of Childcare and Early Years Providers: Main Summary, England, 2019.* Crown Copyright, 2019. (publishing.service.gov.uk).

DfE (2020). Early Years Foundation Stage Profile: 2021 Handbook (EYFS Reforms Early Adopter Version June 2021). Crown Copyright.

DfE (2021). *Statutory Framework for the Early Years Foundation Stage.* Crown Copyright, 2021. (publishing.service.gov.uk).

DfES (2004a). *Choice for Parents, the Best Start for Children: A Ten Year Strategy for Childcare.* HMSO: Crown Copyright.

DfES (2004b). *Every Child Matters: Change for Children.* Nottingham: DfES Publications.

DfES (2006). *Children's Workforce Strategy: Building a World Class Workforce for Children, Young People and Families. The Government Response to the Consultation.* Nottingham: DfES Publications.

DfES (2007). *Governance Guidance for Sure Start Children's Centres and Extended Schools.* Nottingham: DfES Publications, Crown Copyright, 2007.

Dyer, M. A. (2018a). *What does it mean to be an early years practitioner: An investigation into the professional identity of graduate early years practitioners.* Doctoral thesis. University of Huddersfield. http://eprints.hud.ac.uk/id/eprint/34584

Dyer, M. A. (2018b). Being a professional or practising professionally. *European Early Childhood Education Research Journal*, 26 (3), 347–361.

Field, F. (2010). *The Foundation Years: Preventing Poor Children Becoming Poor Adults.* London: Crown Copyright.

Isaacs, S. (1929). *The Nursery Years: The Mind of the Child from Birth to Six Years.* London: Routledge and Kegan Paul.

Katz, L. G. (1985). The nature of professions: Where is early childhood education. Retrieved from ERIC Clearinghouse on Elementary and Early Childhood Education, Urbana, www.eric.ed.gov/?id=ED265948

Lea, S. (2014). Early years work, professionalism and the translation of policy into practice. In: Kingdon, Z. and Gourd, J. (eds.), *Early Years Policy: The Impact on Practice*, 13–32. Abingdon: Routledge.

McGillivray, G. (2008). Nannies, nursery nurses and early years professionals: constructions of professional identity in the early years workforce in England. *European Early Childhood Education Research Journal*, 16 (2), 242–254.

Meering, A. B. (1947). *Handbook for Nursery Nurses.* London: Bailliere, Tindall and Cox.

Moss, P. (2006). Structure, understandings and discourses: Possibilities for re-envisioning the early childhood worker. *Contemporary Issues in Early Childhood*, 7 (1), 30–41.

National Day Nurseries Association (NDNA) (2019). NDNA 2018/19 Workforce Survey England. Huddersfield, 2019.

Nutbrown, C. (2012). *Foundations for Quality: The Independent Review of Early Education and Childcare Qualifications Final Report.* London: Crown Copyright.

Ofsted (2017). *Bold Beginnings: The Reception Curriculum in a Selection of Good and Outstanding Primary Schools.* Manchester: Ofsted.

Osgood, J. (2006). Deconstructing professionalism in early childhood education: Resisting the regulatory gaze. *Contemporary Issues in Early Childhood*, 7 (1), 5–14.

Osgood, J. (2009). Childcare workforce reform in England and 'the early years professional': A critical discourse analysis. *Journal of Education Policy*, 24 (6), 733–751.

Osgood, J. (2010). Reconstructing professionalism in ECEC: The case for the 'critically reflective emotional professional'. *Early Years*, 30 (2), 119–133.

Owen, G. (ed.). (1920). *Nursery School Education*. New York: E. P. Dutton.

Qualifications and Curriculum Authority (QCA)/DfEE (2000). *Curriculum Guidance for the Foundation Stage*. London: QCA and DfEE.

Rumbold, A. (1990). *The Rumbold Report: Starting with Quality*. London: Her Majesty's Stationery Office.

Schon, D. (1983). *The Reflective Practitioner: How Professionals Think in Action*. Aldershot: Ashgate Publishing.

School Curriculum and Assessment Authority (SCAA) (1996). *Desirable Learning Outcomes*. ISBN 0 85522 7737 PP3/33655/498/153.

Sims-Schouten, W. and Strittrich-Lyons, H. (2013). 'Talking the talk': Practical and academic self-concepts of early years practitioners in England. *Journal of Vocational Education and Training*, 66 (1), 39–55.

Skeggs, B. (1988). Gender reproduction and further education: Domestic apprenticeships. *British Journal of Sociology of Education*, 9 (2), 131–149.

Spencer-Woodley, L. (2014). Accountability: Tensions and challenges. In: Kingdon, Z. and Gourd, J. (Eds.), *Early Years Policy: The Impact on Practice*, 33–55. Abingdon: Routledge.

Sure Start (2005). *National Evaluation Report: Early Impacts of Sure Start Local Programmes on Children and Families*. London: HMSO.

West, A. and Noden, P. (2016). *Public Funding of Early Years Education in England: An Historical Perspective Report*. London: Clare Market Papers, LSE. http://eprints.lse.ac.uk/67879

Chapter 2

Professionalisation and the early years workforce

Introduction

This chapter presents a brief history of workforce reform in England and considers key policy drivers which have shaped professionalisation. It goes on to examine workforce professionalisation within an international context of qualifications and roles and discusses the effect of this on the status and agency of practitioners. The chapter explores the problematic divide between education and care and how attempts to dismantle it have failed, threatening professionalisation. Finally, the chapter sets out the steps governments and key stakeholders might take to progress professionalisation, and considers the challenges posed by the public's perception of the practitioner role, workforce involvement in articulating their professional identity and an absence of consistent policy and funding for the sector.

A potted history of workforce reform in England

Graduate-level professional status within the early years workforce is a relatively new phenomenon in England, particularly in the PVI sector. Wright (2011) explains that the PVI sector has been relatively slow to develop, in that the predominant form of early education from 1870 and for 130 years was in state primary schools. This was despite the philanthropic initiatives of church, charitable institutions and individual pioneers such as the McMillan sisters. Maintained nursery provision grew during World War II and subsequently fell, until, in the 1960s, the pre-school movement and voluntary groups began to fill the gap (Wright, 2011). However, even into the 1990s, ECEC services were discretionary, with low levels of public funding (Pugh, 2010) despite the Plowden Report (DES, 1967) highlighting the importance of pre-school provision, and the Children Act 1989 making settings and practitioners accountable for their practice, particularly in relation to child welfare and safety.

Radical reform of the sector and its workforce began with the Labour Government which came to power in 1997 and inherited a system split between early education and day care which Moss (2014, p. 347) describes as 'patchy'. Moss (2014) also asserts that, at that time, England was consistently near the bottom of the European league table for public investment in ECEC, meeting neither demand nor need. During 13 years of the Labour Government, ECEC became a policy priority. In 1998, the Labour Government set targets for the quality and quantity of ECEC in the National Childcare Strategy (NCS), and Osgood (2009) states that, within the policy climate at the time, ECEC was constructed as the crucial means by which full employment, particularly the

DOI: 10.4324/9780367815387-2

employment of mothers, could be achieved. Childcare places increased and significant reform of the workforce began, since at this time the ECEC workforce was largely the domain of working-class women (Osgood, 2005), with low levels of qualification. The government introduced a new national standards and inspection regime and placed much greater emphasis on training and development of the workforce (Pugh, 2010). This commitment to investment in training and developing the workforce was influenced by the findings from the Effective Provision of Pre-School Education (EPPE) (Sylva et al., 2004).

Early childhood education and care policy in England 1998–2010

During the period from 1998 to 2010 the government reiterated the need to radically reform the children's workforce in order to improve employability for parents and outcomes for children. These ideas were promulgated in two key policies: Every Child Matters (ECM) (DfES, 2004a) and the Ten-Year Childcare Strategy (DfES, 2004b). *ECM* (DfES, 2004a) took prevention as its starting point, focusing on entitlements for children, and its long-term vision was the development of integrated health, education and social care through children's centres and extended schools (Pugh, 2014). Contemporaneous with this, the Ten-Year Childcare Strategy (DfES, 2004b) stated that practitioners working with pre-school children should have as much status as a profession as teachers in schools (Reardon, 2009). In 2006, the Childcare Act placed a statutory duty on Local Authorities to take lead responsibility for ECEC; they were given the responsibility to raise quality, improve delivery and achieve better results (HMSO, 2006).

Running parallel to this, the Labour Government demonstrated serious commitment to workforce reform by commissioning a comprehensive review of qualifications and career structures in the sector, culminating in its Children's Workforce Strategy (DfES, 2006). The strategy announced that the newly formed Children's Workforce Development Council (CWDC) would lead on the training and development of the ECEC workforce, and it set out targets for a graduate leader in all children's centres by 2010 and in every PVI setting by 2015. With this goal in mind, the CWDC built on existing foundation degrees and related higher education courses for the ECEC workforce to launch a new graduate status, EYPS (Early Years Professional Status), in 2006 (CWDC, 2006a, 2006b). Assessment for the status was based on 39 standards developed by CWDC (2006c). The Labour Government pledged in excess of £900 million to developing EYPS, with large sums allocated to attracting potential Early Years Professionals (EYPs) and to supporting settings to improve the quality of their provision. This was the first time any English government had pledged such a high level of funding to improving the ECEC sector (Tomlinson, 2013).

Early childhood education and care policy in England 2010–2015

The Labour Government began in a period of economic growth that ended abruptly with the financial crisis of 2007–2008, although spending cuts to children's services did not become a reality until 2011 (Reardon, 2013). The Coalition Government took office in 2010, committed to deficit reduction through cuts to public expenditure. They quickly commissioned a number of independent reviews into children's lives, particularly with respect to health and well-being, education, child protection and the wider impact of poverty on their life chances (Field, 2010; Marmot, 2010; Allen, 2011; Munro, 2011). The Labour Government had also commissioned a review of the EYFS to be carried out by Dame Claire Tickell, and this was published under the Coalition Government in 2011. Subsequently, the findings of these reviews were distilled into one policy document: *Supporting Families in the Foundation Years* (DfE, 2011). In this document the Coalition Government set out their vision for ensuring that all children, whatever their background, should be able to fulfil their potential. It stated, 'It is the child's experiences during the first years that shape their future development and their achievements later in life' (DfE, 2011, p. 2). Therefore, the success of this policy was predicated upon early intervention, where early identification and help were seen as a means to reduce health inequalities, to protect children and to break the cycle of poor outcomes experienced by some children and families. This was reminiscent of the previous government's *ECM* policy (Reardon, 2013), and, in common with *ECM* (DfES, 2004a), it also drew upon research findings from EPPE (Sylva et al., 2004, 2010), indicating a need to support the aspiration for higher-level qualifications for practitioners working with young children. These findings suggested that the quality of practice and provision made a difference, and that there was a positive relationship between the qualifications of staff and ratings of quality (Sylva et al., 2010). Sylva et al. (2010) also found that the greatest impact on quality was when the curriculum leader was a trained teacher, and this was linked specifically with better outcomes in pre-reading and social development at age five.

The Coalition Government continued to focus attention on ECEC and Tickell, in her 2011 review of the EYFS, called on the government to retain the ambition to have a graduate-led workforce in the ECEC sector and recommended greater clarity in identifying career progression routes to EYPS and QTS. In doing so, Tickell (2011) failed to recognise that foundation degrees were already available as a progression route to EYPS. Tickell (2011) also noted that she had heard positive reports about the National Professional Qualification in Integrated Centre Leadership, a qualification specifically for managers of children's centres, but did not draw on evidence provided by Mathers et al. (2011) to endorse EYPS. The review by Mathers et al. (2011) had shown that EYPs were contributing to overall improvements in quality in settings, and adding value in the areas of literacy, planning and inclusion. However, Tickell (2011) drew attention to serious concerns regarding the content and quality of qualifications within the sector, and the continued gender bias in the ECEC workforce. As a result of these concerns, the government commissioned a review of early education and childcare qualifications by Nutbrown.

At the same time, the Coalition Government had set in motion reforms to local government and to public services, including health and education, significantly reducing the number of government quangos (Pugh, 2014). In 2012, CWDC was closed and its programmes of work, including EYPS, were taken over by the Teaching Agency (TA). Moving EYPS from the Children's Workforce Development Council to the Teaching Agency symbolised a change in emphasis for the graduate professional from relational processes, critical reflection and as agents of change to educational outcomes. In addition, when the Coalition Government came to power, only a fraction of the previous funding was announced for the continuation of EYPS as a workforce development strategy (Tomlinson, 2013). Despite the closure of CWDC and the lack of endorsement for EYPS by Tickell (2011), EYPs continued to be identified in the revised EYFS released in March 2012. They were included, alongside qualified teachers, as part of the statutory requirement for staffing arrangements (DfE, 2012), but the ambitious target to have a graduate leader in every PVI setting by 2015 was removed from policy.

Following the publication of the revised EYFS, Nutbrown's review of early education and childcare qualifications was released. Nutbrown (2012) acknowledged the positive impact that EYPS programmes had on individual practitioners and on the quality of settings, whilst pointing out that the lack of parity between EYPS and QTS caused frustration in the sector. This led to a report recommendation, not to strengthen government support for EYPS, but to introduce a specialist early years route to QTS (0–7 years), with an additional conversion qualification being made available to EYPs. There was no similar recommendation for qualified teachers to engage in any additional training, even though their training may have included little knowledge of early child development (0–3 years). Thus, the Nutbrown review simultaneously endorsed EYPS and critiqued it, undermining its specialist knowledge base, thus reinforcing the lack of parity between QTS and EYPS.

In 2013, Truss as Childcare Minister announced the publication of More Great Childcare (DfE, 2013) as a government response to the Nutbrown Review (2012). As a result, the National College for Teaching and Leadership (NCTL) merged with the Teaching Agency (TA) and announced new criteria for Early Years Educator qualifications at Levels 3 and 6, and published Teachers Standards for Early Years, relevant to practitioners working with children aged from birth to five. Thus, Early Years *Professional* Status was replaced by Early Years *Teacher* Status, which, although equivalent to the qualification of the primary school teacher, did not license its holders to work anywhere other than PVI settings. Nutbrown, in 2012, had called for a specialist early years teaching route but, in her response to More Great Childcare, suggested that without QTS,

> Yet again those who work with young children are offered a lesser status, and we should realistically anticipate poorer pay and conditions than those who work with older children.
>
> (Nutbrown, 2013, p. 7)

In 2014 Moss argued that, despite all of the policy initiatives between 1997 and 2014, the old divisions between childcare and education persisted, and even though the position of the workforce had improved somewhat, it remained divided between 'a professional minority and a vast majority of technicians, with the latter still relatively poorly educated and scandalously poorly paid' (p. 354).

The Coalition Government signalled that they continued to support ECEC services in *Supporting Families in the Foundation Years* (DfE/DH, 2011). It introduced funding for free childcare for the most 'vulnerable' two-year-olds and continued to fund places for all three- and four-year-olds (Tomlinson, 2013). Furthermore, in 2015, the Conservative Government pledged to increase the amount of free childcare for working parents from 15 hours per week to 30 hours per week. This equated to a subsidy of 5,000 pounds for parents earning up to 150,000 pounds per year, whilst funding to the sector fell short by 20% (McMahon, 2015). The need for high-quality provision was firmly established at the same time as helping parents back to work, but Kay et al. (2021) argue that economic well-being had become the main driver for early childhood policy, destabilising professionalism, pay, progression and status in the PVI sector.

There were other developments to the education system more broadly including the introduction of academies. Within the academy system, the senior management team has discretion in determining the appropriate qualifications of staff, and in setting their terms and conditions of employment. Significantly, it is no longer necessary for teachers to have QTS to work in an academy (DfE, 2015), and therefore, EYPs and EYTs can seek employment in an academy where pay and conditions may be better than in the PVI sector. However, this does not guarantee that these will match the terms and conditions of their counterparts working in equivalent roles in the maintained education sector.

Early childhood education and care policy in England 2014–2021

This time period is defined by the lack of policy developments regarding professionalisation in the sector, and a fall in the levels of qualified staff, despite considerable expansion in funded ECEC provision. In 2014 entitlement to ECEC for two-year-olds doubled, from being available to the 20% most disadvantaged children to 40% most disadvantaged. In 2015, the entitlement for a funded nursery education place for three- and four-year-olds was extended for the children of eligible working parents from 15 to 30 hours a week. This led to a 4% increase in funded places from 1,386,500 to 1,439,600 and a 9% increase in the workforce (Bonetti, 2020). However, the proportion of practitioners with a Level 3 qualification and higher education diploma fell, and those with a foundation degree or degree remained at 13%. Bonetti (2020) suggests that expansion aims put quantity of ECEC provision ahead of quality, leading to a downward pressure on the level of qualifications.

During this same period, attention arguably moved from a concern about how knowledgeable and qualified practitioners were, to a focus on what their practice should achieve in terms of children's educational outcomes, and how. This move overlooks the relationship between professional education and the quality of practice previously acknowledged in early strategy documents and workforce reform initiatives. However, it could be argued that quality of provision, as measured by its outcomes, was maintained through the use of practice guidance such as Development Matters in the EYFS (Early Education/DfE, 2012; DfE, 2021), the reforming of the EYFS and the Early Learning Goals, and the introduction of an assessment agenda for young children that included the two-year-old check, baseline assessment, phonics tests and the EYFS Profile. The publication by the Office for Standards in Education (Ofsted) of reports about what makes practice effective (Ofsted, 2015, 2017), presented as research studies to inform practice and spark debate and critical reflection within settings, added to this perception that good practice could be codified and modelled across all settings for all children, undermining the need for professional judgement, decisional capital and higher levels of knowledge and understanding in the workforce.

Practice guidance documents and the national assessment agenda for early learning and development have both contributed to a perception that good practice is a matter of compliance rather than critical reflection and professional judgement. The use of guidance documents, framed in such a way as to map out an expected learning and developmental trajectory for all children, arguably undermines the need for higher levels of specialist child development knowledge in the workforce. The timing and content of assessment processes offer opportunity for more knowledgeable professionals to step in and lead interventions to address individual learning needs. The final year of EYFS provision is led by a QTS Reception class teacher (or, in the case of PVI and academy provision, the Level 6 qualified EYT), suggesting that final oversight of early years provision is in expert hands. But this ignores the message from earlier research, that high quality of provision throughout the EYFS is most effectively achieved through a highly qualified workforce, whose practice and judgement can be relied on and trusted.

The Bold Beginnings report (Ofsted, 2017), which sparked heated debate about the importance of play and the quality of the child's experience in ECEC provision up to and including Reception class, has arguably done the most to try to reframe the position and purpose of the EYFS. It characterised the purpose of Reception class, despite its location within the EYFS framework and statutory requirements, as solely to ensure that children had the maths and literacy skills necessary to cope with the new KS1 curriculum, and the social understanding to cope with the formality and regulatory culture of the school. It positioned both the early years practitioner and the EYFS itself as subordinate to the needs of the Year 1 teacher, and accountable for the success and school readiness of the transitioning child. This applies whether the practitioner is the QTS Reception class teacher, or the EYE or EYT leading practice in the PVI pre-school, or even the less qualified Level 2 early years practitioner working under supervision. The emphasis on the success of the child, evidenced through measurable outcomes rather than qualitative assessment and monitoring of their learning, ignores the significantly different minimum qualification standards of the school and PVI sector, and in fact by accepting such variation as a matter of choice made by the PVI employers arguably reinforces the perception that 'proper' learning only takes place in schools, supported and led by 'proper' teachers. Such a perception again undermines the professionalism and identity of the early years workforce in the PVI part of the sector, and is compounded by the withdrawal of such initiatives as the Transformation Fund and graduate-led practice targets.

From September 2021 the new Statutory Framework for the Early Years Foundation Stage (DfE, 2021) has been effective in England, and it contains little guidance to support professionalisation beyond a requirement for appropriate qualifications. However, the new framework heralds reform to the curriculum and practice as it places greater emphasis on readying children for formal learning in Key Stage 1. Potentially the pace of this reform will be speeded up, as the emphasis on readiness for formal learning, particularly in literacy and maths, is likely to be intensified due to concerns that children are falling behind in their learning due to Covid-19. Thus, it is likely that ECEC practitioners will find themselves moving away from a play-based pedagogy to supporting readiness for formal learning and implementing 'catch up' interventions. Whilst it could be argued that this will lessen the divide between education and care it is equally likely that the PVI sector will be viewed as a subordinate feeder to the school system, and the clear definition between early years and Key Stage 1 will be further eroded. Therefore, practitioners may well find that their work receives greater attention and possibly recognition particularly through the inspection process, whilst at the same time they forfeit autonomy and the ethos of ECEC is changed irrevocably.

Arguably, professionalisation of the ECEC workforce in England has stalled, or has even been undermined by the direction of policy and curriculum reform in recent years. In the absence of distinct policy drivers articulating and supporting professionalisation, it is unlikely that reform of the sector as set out in the EYFS (DfE, 2021) and as a result of Covid-19 will be challenged. Campbell-Barr (2018) has argued that this lack of challenge is emblematic of the power inequalities between the 'know and fix' mentality of policymakers, and the views and experiences of ECEC practitioners. This imbalance is particularly relevant in terms of deciding what interventions might be considered appropriate to support young children in early years provision following lockdowns and distanced learning. It is practitioners rather than regulators and policymakers who are with the children every day and therefore better placed to identify their individual needs, but much of the rhetoric of post-Covid catch-up appears to be driven by those external authorities whose considerable power is exercised at some distance from the children and the practitioners themselves. It could be argued that compliance with externally devised interventions is privileged over the professional judgement and decisional capital of the practitioner.

International perspectives on ECEC workforce reform

Vrinioti (2013) draws our attention to the Bologna Process in 1999 as the catalyst to improving the education of early childhood workers across Europe. This trend follows the common and widely accepted assumption that pre-school education is the basis for lifelong learning and that pre-school education, as highlighted in the PISA Study of 2001, had failed to instil positive attitudes to learning in the 15-year-old students surveyed (Vrinioti, 2013). Therefore, across Europe to improve the pre-school system, priority was placed on improving the education of early childhood workers.

However, Oberheumer (2015) points out that professionalisation across Europe is inconsistent due to diverse national constructions and organisational structures of pre-school education, and as Silva (2019) highlights it is problematic to measure what is happening in the 26 member states due to a lack of investment. Moss (2000) reminds us that the approach of each country is developed in line with their dominant constructions of young children and of early childhood workers; hence, there are no universally recognised standards defining professional competence in this field. Nevertheless, Vrinioti (2013) suggests that early childhood workers in contemporary societies are confronted with common problems, leading to similar themes emerging in ECEC, with consequences for professional education and training. This includes increased emphasis on cognitive learning, language acquisition, systematic assessment of children's learning and development, intensive cooperation with parents and children's rights. Vrinioti (2013) argues that, whilst such themes can be used as criteria to develop education and training for early childhood workers, professional competence should also include 'critical reflection upon the conditions under which professional knowledge is applied' (p. 153). Critical reflection, according to Boardman (2020), is integral to Early Years Teacher Status in England, linking leadership, professionalism and quality. Although, across Europe, more generally leadership is not one of the emerging themes in professional competence (Vrinioti, 2013).

The education–care divide

The work of the Organisation for Economic Co-operation and Development (OECD) (2012) appears to show that it is a widely held view internationally that educating young children is distinct from caring for young children and that it requires higher levels of knowledge and skill. The OECD (2012) found that, generally, practitioners associated with delivering early education, such as pre-school teachers, had higher initial qualifications than care staff. They also found that more professional development opportunities are available for teachers than care staff. Consequently, the OECD (2012) recommended that there was a need for governments to think beyond curriculum dichotomies and that this should be extended to the split between education and care.

There have been attempts to unify care and education in some European countries including England through the introduction of EYFS, although disparities in status and pay persist. Italy has made attempts to integrate their previously split system of education and care (Silva, 2019) by linking in law ECEC services with primary schools. They have also introduced precise qualifications at degree level for ECEC educators and pedagogical coordinators at master's level. The pedagogical coordinator has taken a lead role in turning infant schools focused on care into educational organisations in the integrated birth to six system in Italy, and Silva (2019, p. 384) describes their role as 'professionalism with sundry functions.' However, as Silva (2019) points out there are regional variations in Italy, ECEC provision is patchy and the role of the pedagogical coordinator is not uniformly defined.

Vrinioti (2013) argues that in Greece there is also a split system of care and education. Some universities have been offering academic studies for pre-school pedagogues for more than 25 years, but the focus is normally on working with children aged between four and six years. Crucially the education of those students aiming to work with pre-schoolers in some parts of Greece is very different from that of students being educated for primary and secondary teaching, possibly intensifying the divide between practitioners working in the pre-school sector and later sectors of education (Vrinioti, 2013).

Oberheumer (2015) explains that in some areas of Germany significant reforms have taken place in linking ECEC and primary schools by introducing an integrated framework from birth to 10 years old. Also strongly influenced by the European Qualifications Framework they raised the level of formal qualification requirements for working with young children to degree level. However, in 2013 the Federal Ministry for Education placed the traditional vocational post-secondary qualification at the same level as the degree on the German Qualification Framework, and this was judged to be a step backwards in the professionalisation project (Oberheumer, 2015). Nevertheless, Germany is committed to professionalisation of the ECEC workforce signified in the Early Years Professional Development Initiative which funds research, staff development and a professional network.

Beyond Europe

Policy initiatives to improve the quality of education and care through workforce development have been ongoing in New Zealand since 1986 (Cherrington and Thornton, 2013). Dalli (2008) points out that England looked to New Zealand as one of the countries leading the way in creating a professionalised workforce for ECEC. Diverse provision exists at service level in New Zealand, and settings are licensed as either teacher led or parent led. Parent-led services are predominantly play centres or Maori language nests, and teacher-led services include kindergartens, education and care services and home-based services (New Zealand Gov, n.d.). Warren (2014) argues that education reforms in the country brought ECEC under the education umbrella in the Early Childhood Education (ECE) Strategic Plan 2002 so the separation between care and education was removed. The same professional standards were introduced for ECEC teachers as for primary and secondary, and there was a requirement for 100% registered teachers in teacher-led services by 2012; this target has since been revised to 80% (Cherrington and Thornton, 2013). However, Stuart (2020) states that teachers working in ECEC in New Zealand are still viewed as less professional than their colleagues in the compulsory sector, as they are considered to be outside the norm as modelled on the classroom.

Internationally there are moves towards raising the levels of qualification of the ECEC workforce, however, as the OECD (2019) found the trend towards a three-year degree is for those with responsibility for pre-school children, whilst those working with infants and toddlers tend towards lower levels of qualification and training. The OECD (2019) also noted that low pay and status and poor working conditions remained a concern, and arguably this might explain why retention of higher qualified staff is identified as a major challenge (Bonetti, 2019; OECD, 2019). Martin et al. (2020), in their research in Australia, found that there was an intention to recognise ECEC as a profession ten years ago in the Early Years Learning Framework by requiring all providers to designate, in writing, an educational leader, and initially it was intended that the educational leader would hold a four-year degree. However, in some regions as many as 25% of settings have been unable to recruit, forcing a change in policy to allow a suitably qualified and experienced practitioner to step into the role (Martin et al., 2020).

Vandenbroeck et al. (2013) criticise an imposed model of professionalism as seen in England and across a range of countries. They argue that that the transnational framework of competencies, argued for in the Bologna declaration, leads to a narrow technical professionalism, rather than a reflective professionalism. Hordern (2013) also argues that when practitioners lack control over the body of knowledge that defines their practice, and the pace of reform, this leads to ongoing dependence on government and the more dominant 'welfare professions such as teaching and social work for validation of this model of professionalism' (p. 107).

This review of some international perspectives of professionalisation in ECEC shows that it is progressing across a range of countries including Italy, Germany, Greece, New Zealand, Australia and England. However, it appears that in most of the countries disparity between education and care persists and this leads to a lack of parity in status, pay and working conditions between those working in education and those caring for young children.

Moving professionalisation forward

In England Bonetti (2020) has called for the government to revive the Early Years Workforce Strategy to provide a long-term overarching framework and funding to tackle deep-rooted systemic issues in the workforce. These issues include the classed and gendered nature of the workforce and the historic split between education and care which result in the low status, low pay and poor working conditions of the sector. To date these issues have shown themselves to be stubborn and not easily eradicated; they would require consistent and persistent policy directives and funding. In addition, she recommends a comprehensive workforce registry detailing qualifications, training and professional development to help individual practitioners, settings and government to monitor workforce trends and plan professional development opportunities.

Across Europe the OECD (2019) have identified eight steps that governments can take to support professionalisation. These include:

• promote the status of the profession
• improve pay
• implement strategies to boost qualifications
• increase the emphasis on practical training and induction training

- provide alternative routes into the profession
- extend efforts to recruit men into the profession
- improve working conditions
- strengthen policies to encourage in-service training and continuing professional development.

These steps are not new and underpinned policy developments in England for a period of 15 years from 1998. However, 15 years of policy interest was not enough to overturn centuries of policy inertia and lack of investment. Furthermore, what is missing from these recommendations to support professionalisation are the voices of significant stakeholders including parents and the workforce.

Stakeholder participation in professionalisation

There are many stakeholders with a potential interest and part to play in professionalisation of the ECEC workforce. The whole of society benefits from happy, healthy and educated children, but parents are considered to be powerful stakeholders with a close and immediate interest in who is educating and caring for their children. Chen and Bradbury (2020) found that parents tend not to consider staff qualifications and training when selecting ECEC, and this is because they have limited choice due to practical considerations. Most parents have to prioritise convenience and availability, and when parents take quality into consideration they tend to focus on the personality and attitude of practitioners. Chen and Bradbury (2020) point out that further investigation is needed to understand parental awareness of quality in ECEC and how this benefits children. Arguably if parents were fully aware of the association between quality, levels of practitioner qualifications and children's outcomes parental choice would become an active stimulant for provider quality, and driver of professionalisation.

In the market economy the PVI sector is serving the needs of children and their parents so if parents have little interest in the professional qualifications of staff, it follows that professionalisation through higher-level qualifications will not be a priority for the sector. Furthermore, the paradox at the heart of professionalisation of the ECEC workforce is that professionalism is intrinsically linked to a high degree of autonomy and control over one's work, whilst increasingly being mandated by 'top down' government policy intervention (Havnes, 2018) particularly the more formal early years curriculum in England, which potentially undermines professionalisation for the workforce. As Dyer (2018) points out other professions are able to define their practice to a greater extent than practitioners in ECEC, and Havnes (2018) also recognises the need for practitioners to have a greater say in articulating their professional knowledge and standards. Practitioners privilege relationships within and beyond the setting and children's social and emotional development in their model of professionalism; however, they lack the confidence to draw upon and articulate a critical understanding of theory and research which underpins their practice (Dyer, 2018). There is a complex interplay of factors which undermines their confidence, including low status and social capital, absence of a unified voice due to the fragmented and diverse workforce, and a poorly conceptualised early years pedagogy which centres on an individual ethic of care. Dyer (2018) argues that the workforce requires a transformative education which includes critical examination of how they might work together across the sector and recognise that they share responsibility for having their voice heard.

Higher education institutions (HEIs) are also significant stakeholders through research which shapes practice and previously influenced policy, and because many post-1992 universities offer a range of degree-level programmes which are benchmarked against sector-specific occupational standards, including Teaching Standards Early Years, Early Years Educator at Level 6 and most recently the Graduate Practitioner Standards developed by the Early Childhood Studies Degree Network. Tensions are inherent in these programmes which expect students and practitioners, through the process of reflection, to challenge and question policy and practice, whilst simultaneously adhering to the demands of the curriculum and how it is implemented in the setting and meeting occupational standards. These tensions can make it difficult for students and practitioners to feel secure with their developing professional identity. In addition, many graduates of these programmes use them as a progression route into a postgraduate teaching course due to the lack of a coherent career structure, status and poor pay associated with a graduate role in the PVI sector; therefore, their association with ECEC is often transient. From 2004 until 2010 funding to the Local Authority (LA) from the Graduate Leader Fund and to the HEI for EYPS enabled graduate professional networks to be established. As part of one of these networks tutors, students, graduate practitioners and representatives from the LA became a professional community participating in a range of professional development opportunities including small research projects and visits to centres of excellence such as Penn Green. These networks, although briefly, facilitated collective working and opportunities for graduate professionals to have their voice heard. Unfortunately, substantial cuts to LA funding and low levels of recruitment in HEIs, particularly to EYTS programmes (Bonetti, 2019), mean that resources are no longer available to support this type of professional network. In addition, HEIs are operating in a market economy where individual tutors are required to manage many competing demands which inevitably draw their attention and energy away from driving forward professionalisation in the sector.

Professional status is based on public recognition of the value of services on offer (Evetts, 2003) and increasingly relies on agreement or a 'professional mandate' (Whitty, 2008, p. 32) with the state and stakeholders. Unfortunately, the required public recognition and stakeholder support have not yet been achieved for professional status to be firmly established in the ECEC workforce, due in part to confusion over what the role of the early years practitioner actually is. The problematic divide between education and care remains a significant challenge to any professionalisation project in England and internationally, despite a number of governments trying to integrate ECEC with primary education through a common curriculum framework. Even though practitioners in ECEC are working within the same curriculum and regulatory framework as their colleagues in primary education, there is a lack of parity in pay, and opportunities for career progression. To address this would require considerable and collective effort from all stakeholders and government, and a long-term funding commitment.

Conclusion

The policy landscape then, nationally and internationally, from 1998 to 2010 was instrumental in driving forward professionalisation of the ECEC workforce. However, this remained a one dimensional, 'from above' (Evetts, 2003) approach to workforce reform, based solely on the development of individual human capital, and accepted and engaged with by early years practitioners. In England, the Labour Government committed high levels of investment in transforming the sector through the Graduate Leader Fund, which was successful in raising the levels of qualifications of the workforce and improving the accessibility and quality of provision. However, there was no similar improvement to the pay, working conditions and status of the workforce. There then followed a period of austerity, funding dried up and policy fragmented, and commitment to professionalisation waned. From 2014 the government's focus has been on increasing the number of ECEC places and bringing the early years framework closer to the more formal curriculum in Key Stage 1. Seemingly professionalisation is no longer part of the policy landscape in England, and the claiming of professional status and identity now lies in the hands of a diverse and fragmented workforce employed in a myriad of small organisations, with no infrastructure to support the development of a collective voice. Arguably professionalisation has stalled and a collective effort from the government and key stakeholders is needed to drive it forward which will require a long-term commitment in policy and funding. The following chapter discusses where the workforce reform agenda now leaves the early years practitioner and offers theoretical frameworks for understanding how they understand and accept their identity and status.

References

Allen, G. (2011). *Early Intervention: The Next Steps*. London: Crown Publications.

Boardman, K. (2020). Early years teachers as leaders of change through reflexivity praxis? *Early Child Development and Care*, 190 (3), 322–332.

Bonetti, S. (2019). The early years workforce in England: A comparative analysis using the Labour Force Survey. Education Policy Institute and Nuffield Foundation.

Bonetti, S. (2020). Early years workforce development in England: Key ingredients and missed opportunities. Education Policy Institute and Nuffield Foundation.

Campbell-Barr, V. (2018). The silencing of the knowledge-base in early childhood education and care professionalism. *International Journal of Early Years Education*, 26 (1), 75–89. https://doi.org/10.1080/09669760.2017.1414689

Chen, H. and Bradbury, A. (2020). Parental choice of childcare in England: Choosing in Phases and the split market. *British Educational Research Journal*, 46 (2), 281–300.

Cherrington, S. and Thornton, K. (2013). Continuing professional development in early childhood education in New Zealand. *Early Years*, 33 (2), 119–132.

Children's Workforce Development Council (CWDC) (2006a). *Early Years Professional Prospectus*. Leeds: CWDC.

Children's Workforce Development Council (CWDC) (2006b). *A Head Start for All*. London, CWDC.

Children's Workforce Development Council (CWDC) (2006c). *Early Years Professional National Standards*. [online] Last accessed 15/3/2022 http://www.lancsngfl.ac.uk/curriculum/early_years/download/file/Draft_EYP_Standards_Aug_2006.pdf

Dalli, C. (2008). Pedagogy, knowledge and collaboration: Towards a ground-up perspective on professionalism. *European Early Childhood Education Research Journal*, 16 (2), 171–185.

Department for Education (DfE) (2011). *Supporting Families in the Foundation Years*. Crown Publications. [online] Last accessed 10/3/22 www.gov.uk

Department for Education (DfE) (2012). *Statutory Framework for the Early Years Foundation Stage: Setting the Standards for Learning, Development and Care for Children from Birth to Five*. [online] Last accessed 10/3/22 http://www.foundationyears.org.uk/files/2014/05/eyfs_statutory_framework_march_2012.pdf

Department for Education (DfE) (2013). *More Great Childcare: Raising Quality and Giving Parents More Choice.* [online] Last accessed 10/3/22 Department for Education - (publishing. service.gov.uk)

Department for Education (DfE) (2015). *2010 to 2015 Government Policy Academies and Free Schools.*

Department for Education and Science (DES) (1967). *The Plowden Report: Children and their Primary Schools.* London: HMSO.

Department for Education and Skills (DfES) (2004a). *Every Child Matters: Change for Children.* London: HMSO.

Department for Education and Skills (DfES) (2004b). *Ten Year Childcare Strategy-Choice for Parents: The Best Start for Children.* London: HMSO.

Department for Education and Skills (DfES) (2006). *Children's Workforce Strategy: Building a World Class Workforce for Children, Young People and Families. The Government response to the consultation.* Nottingham: DfES Publications.

DfE (2021). *Statutory Framework for the Early Years Foundation Stage.* Crown Copyright, 2021.

Dyer, M. (2018). Being a professional or acting professionally. *European Early Childhood Education Research Journal,* 26 (3), 347–361.

Early Education/DfE (2012). *Development Matters in the Early Years Foundation Stage.* London: Crown Copyright.

Evetts, J. (2003). The sociological analysis of professionalism: Occupational change in the modern world. *International Sociology,* 18(2), 395–415. https://doi.org/10.1177/0268580903018002005

Field, F. (2010). *The Foundation Years: Preventing Poor Children Becoming Poor Adults.* London: Cabinet Office.

Havnes, A. (2018). ECEC professionalisation-challenges of developing professional standards. *European Early Childhood Education Research Journal,* 26 (5), 657–673.

Her Majesty's Stationery Office (HMSO) (2006). *The Childcare Act.* London: HMSO.

Hordern, J. (2013). A productive system of early years professional development. *Early Years,* 33 (2), 106–118.

Kay, L., Wood, E., Nuttall, J. and Henderson, L. (2021). Problematising policies for workforce reform in early childhood education: A rhetorical analysis of England's Early Years Teacher Status. *Journal of Education Policy,* 36 (2), 179–195. https://doi.org/10.1080/02680939.2019.1637546

Marmot, M. (2010). *Fair Society: Healthy Lives.* UCL Last accessed 25/7/22 https://www.instituteofhealthequity.org/resources-reports/fair-society-healthy-lives-the-marmot-review/fair-society-healthy-lives-full-report-pdf.pdf

Martin, J., Nuttall, J., Henderson, L. and Wood, E. (2020). Educational leaders and the project of professionalisation in early childhood education in Australia. *International Journal of Educational Research,* 101, 101559. https://doi.org/10.1016/j.ijer.2020.101559

Mathers, S., Ranns, H., Karemaker, A., Moody, A., Sylva K., Graham, J. and Siraj-Blatchford, I. (2011). *Evaluation of the Graduate Leader Fund Final Report.* DfE [online] Last accessed 25/7/22 publishing.service.gov.uk

McMahon, S. (2015). *Free Childcare Won't Be as Easy as ABC.* [online] Last accessed 25/7/22 https://childcarecanada.org/documents/child-care-news/15/06/increasing-free-childcare-wont-be-easy-b-c

Moss, P. (2000). Training of early childhood education and care staff. *International Journal of Educational Research,* 33 (1), 31–53.

Moss, P. (2014). Early childhood policy in England 1997–2013: Anatomy of a missed opportunity. *International Journal of Early Years Education,* 22 (4), 346–358.

Munro, E. (2011). *The Munro Review of Child Protection: Final Report- A Child Centred System.* London: Crown Publications. [online] Last accessed 10/3/22 https://www.education.gov.uk/publications/standard/publicationDetail/Page1/CM%208062

New Zealand Government Childcare and Preschool in New Zealand (n.d.). [online] Last accessed 25/7/22 https://www.live-work.immigration.govt.nz/live-in-new-zealand/education-and-schooling/preschool-care-and-education

Nutbrown, C. (2012). *Foundations for Quality: The Independent Review of Early Education and Child Care Qualifications*. London: Crown Publications. [online] Last accessed 25/7/22 https://www.gov.uk/government/publications/nutbrown-review-foundations-for-quality

Nutbrown, C. (2013). *Shaking the Foundations of Quality? Why Childcare 'Policy' Must Not Lead to Poor Quality Early Education and Care*. Sheffield: University of Sheffield.

Oberhuemer, P. (2015). Parallel discourses with unparalleled effects: Early years workforce development and professionalisation initiatives in Germany. *International Journal of Early Years Education*, 23 (3), 303–312. https://doi.org/10.1080/09669760.2015.1074560

Ofsted (2015). *Early Years: The Report of Her Majesty's Chief Inspector of Education, Children's Services and Skills, 2015*. London: Crown Copyright.

Ofsted (2017). *Bold Beginnings: The Reception Curriculum in a Selection of Good and Outstanding Primary Schools*. Manchester: Ofsted.

Organisation For Economic Cooperation and Development (OECD) (2012). *Starting Strong 111: A Quality Toolkit for Early Childhood Education and Care*. [online] Last accessed 11/3/22 https://www.oecd.org/education/school/startingstrongiii-aqualitytoolboxforearlychildhoodeducationandcare.htm

Organisation for Economic Cooperation and Development (OECD) (2019). Leadership for Quality Early Childhood Education and Care: OECD Education Working Paper No. 211. [online] Last accessed 11/3/22 https://www.oecd.org/officialdocuments/publicdisplaydocumentpdf/?cote=EDU/WKP(2019)19&docLanguage=En

Osgood, J. (2005). Who cares? The classed nature of childcare. *Gender and Education*, 7 (3), 289–303.

Osgood, J. (2009). 'Childcare workforce reform in England and the' early years professional': A critical discourse analysis. *Journal of Education Policy*, 24 (6), 733–751.

Pugh, G. (2010). The policy Agenda for early childhood services. In: Pugh, G. and Duffy, B. (eds.), *Contemporary Issues in the Early Years* (5th ed.). London: Sage, 7–21.

Pugh, G. (2014). The policy Agenda for early childhood services. In: Pugh, G. and Duffy, B. (eds.), *Contemporary Issues in the Early Years* (6th ed.), 3–21. London: Sage.

Reardon, D. (2009). *Achieving Early Years Professional Status*. London: Sage.

Reardon, D. (2013). *Achieving Early Years Professional Status* (2nd ed.). London: Sage.

Silva, C. (2019). The professionalization of early childhood education, care educators and pedagogical coordinators: A key issue of adult education. *Form@re*, 19 (2), 377. https://doi.org/10.13128/formare-25249

Stuart, M. (2020). Being professional in New Zealand early childhood education: A genealogy. *Policy Futures in Education*, 18 (5), 597–609. https://doi.org/10.1177/1478210319875577

Sylva, K., Melhuish, E., Sammons, P., Siraj-Blatchford, I. and Taggart, B. (2010). *Early Childhood Matters: Evidence from the Effective Pre-School and Primary Education Project*. Oxon: Routledge.

Sylva, K., Melhuish, P., Sammons, I., Siraj-Blatchford, I. and Taggart, B. (2004). *The Effective Provision of Pre-School Education Project; Findings from the Pre-School Period*. London: DfES.

Tickell, C. (2011). *The Early Years Foundations for Life, Health and Learning. An Independent Report on the Early Years Foundation Stage to Her Majesty's Government*. London: DfE.

Tomlinson, P. (2013). *Early Years Policy and Practice: A Critical Alliance*. Northwich: Critical Publishing.

Vandenbroeck, M., Peeters, J. and Bouverne-De-Bie, M. (2013). Lifelong learning and counter / professionalisation of childcare: A case study of local hybridizations of global European discourses. *European Early Childhood Education Research Journal*, 21 (1), 109–124.

Vrinioti, K. (2013). Professionalisation in early childhood education: A comparative view of emerging. *European Early Childhood Education Research Journal*, 21 (1), 150–163.

Warren, A. (2014). How do newly qualified early childhood teachers in Aotearoa New Zealand critically reflect within constraints and possibilities of dominant discourses of early childhood teaching? *International Research in Early Childhood Education*, 5 (1), 124–139.

Whitty, G. (2008). Changing modes of teacher professionalism: Traditional, managerial, collaborative and democratic. In: Cunningham, B. (ed.) *Exploring Professionalism*, 144–160. London: Bedford Way Papers.

Wright, H. (2011). *Women Studying Childcare: Integrating Lives through Adult Education.* Stoke, Trentham Books.

Chapter 3

Constructing a professional identity, claiming professional agency

Introduction

Workforce reform initiatives for the early years sector and the development of the practitioner role have been driven by a perception of this workforce as lacking at a personal or individual level, i.e. lacking in skills and knowledge, a deficit view that has been addressed by providing funding and opportunities for access to training and professional education. However, Hargreaves and Fullan (2012) argue that professionalism in education comprises not only of such an increase in human capital, but also the development of social and decisional capital – the ability to influence and interact with others, and to exercise one's own judgement in a professional context. Thus, the formation of professional identity relies not only on the educational opportunities made available to the individual, but also on the social context of their work, the infrastructure of the professional field and having the autonomy to act according to their values and experiences, and by doing so, to contribute to the shaping of their professional context. An identity framed solely in terms of what the individual knows and how this is applied within the confines of an externally regulated professional framework will be limited in terms of agency and self-determination.

This chapter explores theoretical frameworks that propose explanations for how the individual constructs their identity, and how these indicate a symbiotic relationship between an individual and their social, cultural and historical context, how they define themselves and how social, cultural or political factors shape this perception. These theories do not simply position the individual as subject to the influence of external forces and perceptions, but also argue that as individuals, it is our own acceptance or challenge of such pressure that gives or withholds power to these forces. Identity is understood as a dynamic construct, changing and developing in response to social, cultural and political change, and in response to an individual's growing awareness of his or her own values in relation to these factors.

The construction of identity

Burr (2015) argues that we construct knowledge and understanding of our world through our interactions and relationships with others around us, implying that our understanding of identity results from how others see us, how we see ourselves in relation to these perceptions and the extent to which we accept or challenge them. She goes on to propose that our understanding of identity is shaped by dominant cultural discourse, and by the purpose of the identified object or person, in the eyes of the beholder. Most particularly,

DOI: 10.4324/9780367815387-3

it is the perceptions of those with the greatest authority or control within a social context who have the power to shape the identity of an individual, and it is the capacity of the individual to challenge this that determines how easily this identity is accepted. This is especially important in the determination of a professional identity that includes making judgements about appropriate and best practice, in a role based on forming a network of varied relationships with service users, regulators, employers and young children, and that is intended to promote the development and well-being of others.

Theoretical frameworks that set out how identity may be constructed go further in explaining how power and status play an active and significant role in shaping identity, both at a personal and a professional level. Foucault's work on self-formation offers insight into how practitioners themselves use mechanisms within their social world, and the perception of others, to frame an identity and a role. Bourdieu (Bourdieu and Passeron, 1990; Bourdieu and Wacquant, 1992) argues that power and relationships within a field, or social context, influence how we make sense of our social world and our own place in it. Bronfenbrenner's ecological model of development (Bronfenbrenner, 1979, 1986), setting out a number of different systems that comprise an individual's environment, also offers a context for understanding how a sense of identity can be influenced and developed. These theoretical frameworks construct identity as a dynamic concept formed through interactions and relationships with others, and consider where the power to influence and shape development lies. By raising awareness of the processes and forces that shape how individuals perceive their role and place within a social or cultural framework, this then offers insight into how they can be empowered to make their own decisions about whether to comply with these pressures or challenge them.

Foucault

Foucault (1982, cited in Rabinow, 1984) argues that individuals are empowered through a combination of knowledge and practice, but for early years practitioners, this emphasis on the disposition and compliance of the practitioner arguably restricts their autonomy to interpret knowledge and apply it to their practice. Where practice and knowledge are externally controlled and limited in this way, so the power of the individual will be shaped and contained. Foucault's social construction of human nature, who we are, can be used to develop a specific understanding of practice, i.e. what we do. Therefore, the identity of the practitioner in terms of what they do presents a construction of early years practice, which in turn perpetuates a social understanding of the role and status of the practitioner, which goes on to influence how practitioners sees themselves. This relationship between the identity of the practitioner and the nature and status of their practice is demonstrated in the historical and gendered perception of the practitioner as maternal and nurturing, leading to a discourse of practice centred on care, and understood as requiring little to no education (Moss, 2006), but rather an appropriate disposition. The vocational habitus (Colley et al., 2003) of the practitioner, derived through their initial vocational education and their lack of social and cultural capital, further supports this emphasis on the right nature for the role (rather than more intellectual qualifications or attributes), offering social approval for this in the place of more long-term or tangible forms of capital reward (Colley, 2006). It is by questioning and examining how the nature or personal disposition of the practitioner is used so successfully within this relationship that it becomes possible to understand how their identity, and their habitus, are formed and perpetuated, and also how these might be challenged.

Foucault identifies three ways in which the individual self is defined or objectified, through rules that determine who does what, how individuals are identified and categorised, and how they explain and identify themselves. These processes share a strong emphasis on practice underpinned by knowledge, set within accepted social structures that determine the boundaries of legitimate behaviour. Within the early years sector, these mechanisms also draw on the nature of the practitioner and their compliance with externally set restrictions on their role.

Dividing practices (Foucault (1982), cited in Rabinow (1984)), are the means by which individuals (for example those who work with young children) are objectified or dehumanised into a category or classification (the early years practitioner and their varying levels of qualification) and separated from other specific groups of individuals. These can be used to determine who is allowed to work where and with what level of oversight and autonomy, and define an appropriate environment for what constitutes an early years setting. External authorities – which include the DfE sponsored regulating body Ofsted – judge the appropriateness of the environment and define the type of provision that can be offered. The language of regulation continues to focus on disposition and moral character, including such dogmatic phrases as *fit persons*, to indicate by implication that there are *unfit*, rather than simply unqualified or unknowledgeable, persons in society to hold such jobs.

The scientific classification (Foucault (1982), cited in Rabinow (1984)) of the practitioner has equally contributed to their professional identity, and the debate about the role or purpose of the practitioner. Early job titles reflected an emphasis on children's care and well-being – nursery nurse, child-minder, nanny – whilst more modern equivalents reflected an attempt to capture the uniqueness of the role – early years assistant, practitioner, professional. However, these newer titles said little about what the job role was, other than it being associated with young children, as did apparently neutral terms such as 'crèche worker' and 'nursery assistant'. While these titles and classifications could be structured into hierarchies within specific organisations, none of them offer much guidance as to the required knowledge or skills base for these roles across the workforce and the sector. The inclusion of levels of qualification (NVQ Level 2 and 3 for example) remain unhelpful for the outsider as they do not sufficiently describe the place or nature of the role. Consequently, parents, teachers, health professionals and early years practitioners themselves have continued to have a varied understanding of what is required of a competent practitioner and what level of qualification, knowledge or skill they need (Nutbrown, 2012). In particular, this has left parents to form an understanding of the role of the practitioner in terms of their own experience, and their interactions and relationships with their children, i.e. based on personal dispositions and nature, rather than knowledge and understanding. This has impacted on how practitioners refer to themselves, so that their job titles more often reflect public perception of their role rather than any claim to greater status, educational role or expertise:

> I've been called a nursery nurse, nursery office ... people understand automatically if you say nursery nurse.
>
> (Gail)

> [I call myself] an early years practitioner, but I normally need to explain then a nursery nurse.
>
> (Meg)

I always call myself a registered [emphasised] childminder ... so people know it's an official capacity and it's a real job.

(Alice)

I probably say a nursery nurse ... it's a comforting name for parents ... and if you said early years practitioner they might think that you are better than what you are.

(Claire)

The title of teacher has continued to be reserved for those with postgraduate QTS qualifications, licensed to work in the compulsory education sector. The introduction of more educationally related job roles (Early Years Educator, Early Years Teacher Status) now reflects the responsibility of the practitioner to secure young children's educational outcomes. However, in designating these titles as Early Years roles, this clearly marks the limited scope of their currency, setting them apart from, and potentially subordinate to, those simply designated as teachers. For example, Penny describes herself as 'an early years teacher ... I am not classed as a nursery teacher', meaning that she does not have the Qualified Teacher Status (QTS) that her colleagues running Reception class and Key Stage have. Framing them as *equivalent to* teachers, rather than the *same as* teachers, continues the implication that there is a boundary between the two roles, perpetuated by restrictions on where graduate practitioners could work, and the differences in terms and conditions of employment they experienced (Kay et al., 2021). Foucauldian analysis would argue that we clearly and successfully classify the early years workforce as individuals whose employment and remit are strictly limited to children under five, most often in pre-school provision, and with no leading role or responsibility within the compulsory sector.

Practitioners' subjectification or self-formation – 'a process of self-understanding but one which is mediated by an external authority figure' (Foucault (1982), cited in Rabinow (1984), p. 11) – underpins how many within the early years workforce define themselves, and similarly reflects an emphasis on nature and disposition. Practitioners emphasise the practical nature of how they care for young children, or contribute to their learning, their development, their general well-being in terms of health, safety and emotional development (Sims-Schouten and Strittrich-Lyons, 2013). For example, Nina's explanation of the role of the Key Person, a mandatory welfare requirement to support children's social and emotional development, prioritises the practical and relational elements of the role rather than the understanding and application of psychological theory to practice:

They [the key person] do all the nappies, ... they're involved with the parents ... they are there for the children, they sit with them at dinnertime, they fill in all their daily diaries, they've got a relationship with them [the child] and the parents.

(Nina)

But in defining their role, they draw on dividing practices and scientific classifications to clarify what they are, and are not, allowed to be, rather than emphasising the unique expertise and specialism of their role. They are **not** teachers, health professionals or social workers. They refer to regulatory frameworks and levels of qualification to define their role – as *Ofsted recognised* early years practitioners; as *Level 2 or 3 qualified* practitioners; as *registered* child-minders; and those with Early Years Professional or Early

Years Teacher Status claim equivalence with a nursery teacher with QTS, but in doing so, set themselves apart from this specific job title.

These three mechanisms demonstrate how external regulatory frameworks along with control over the curriculum and pedagogy of vocational training for early years practitioners can significantly influence their professional practice and identity. Despite sharing a knowledge base with teachers, midwives and health visitors in particular, the location of their practice defines the identity of the early years practitioner, and even limits their claim to status as professionals. Both the dividing practices and the scientific classifications identified here combine to give shape to Bourdieu's concept of field for the early years sector, whilst scientific classification along with self-subjectification combines to underpin the habitus, including vocation habitus, of the practitioner. This reliance on external frameworks and authority to understand one's own identity and value arguably undermines the workforce's confidence and power in determining for themselves what their role is or what standards they should be meeting. Establishing a professional identity through the disposition and practical attributes of the practitioner, rather than their acquisition of and critical reflection on a specialist knowledge base applied to practice, can be compounded by a lack of collective voice on the part of the workforce to determine for themselves how they should be perceived (Hordern, 2016). The lack of an 'internal' authority such as a General Council or Royal College, formed from *within* the workforce to support the workforce, may well be what keeps the early years sector bound to a set of definitions of what they are not and what they lack, or what they are only in relation to other professions, and limits their power within their field of practice.

Bourdieu and the early years workforce

Bourdieu's account of identity (Bourdieu and Wacquant 1992) focuses on a social world where relationships and interactions within a field are shaped by the power individuals can draw from their social and cultural capital. From this we develop a habitus, a set of structuring structures (Bourdieu, 1977) that determine how we behave, and how we perceive ourselves and accept our place in relation to others. In presenting field and habitus as representing 'bundles of relations' (Wacquant, in Bourdieu and Wacquant, 1992, p. 16), these concepts can be understood as demonstrated through interactions, or processes determined by those who hold power in a social field, rather than as overt structures or rules. This includes, in a very real sense, the unwritten rules of engagement across the sector about who has a relationship with whom, and the nature of the relationships between policymakers and providers, or inspectors and practitioners, or practitioners and academic writers and researchers.

Bourdieu and Passeron (1990) further argue that powerful élites impose hegemonic discourses through social institutions, particularly education systems, in order to maintain and perpetuate control of power and capital. This implies that the identity and role of the early years practitioner is defined by society in general, and their vocational trainers and regulators or policymakers in particular. Acceptance of these power relations is what drives the development of habitus, which further reinforces the structure of the field. The construction of identity and role is dependent on the power of the individual to effect change across a field, so that individual action, personal values, ethics or understanding will have little effect if not tied to power. This suggests that for those in a subordinate position within a field, their identity and agency are determined not only through their relatively limited power but also by their acceptance of this position. Whilst it is clear how this applies to the early years practitioner, it applies equally to those who own and manage provision organised into small to medium enterprises, who are subject to government regulation and quality assurance to maintain access to government subsidies and funding, to ensure the sustainability of their services. Thus in considering the development and role of both field and habitus for the early years practitioner, Bourdieu's concepts again demonstrate a cyclical relationship, this time between how practitioners and providers see and position themselves in relation to external authorities, how this reinforces the power of those controlling authorities and how it shapes and is shaped by broader social perceptions of their role and status.

Bourdieu argues that change will occur within a field only when it is driven by those with power, and such change will disrupt, for a time, the habitus of individual actors. Government, through its policy and the development of the sector's regulatory framework, is an extremely powerful actor in this field, despite being at the periphery of practice that largely takes place in privately owned provision. The 1998 Childcare Strategy (DfEE, 1998) identified the needs of working parents as a key driver in the expansion of the sector, positioning parents as consumers and provision as a commodity to be retailed. The development of Sure Start Local Programmes and Children's Centres introduced a discourse of early invention to support children's development, arguably re-defining the relationship between practitioner and parent. The introduction of the EYFS in 2008 positioned all registered early years providers as educators of young children, whether they were in receipt of nursery education funding or not, and required them to acknowledge this in the planning of their practice. At the same time, all registered settings, including school-based nursery and Reception classes, were required to practice to the same set of overarching principles that included respect for the uniqueness of the individual child and the importance of positive and affectionate relationships to support learning. Whilst this might imply change in approaches to practice for both education and care provision, the fact that workforce reform strategies (DfES, 2005, 2006; DfE, 2017) focused on increasing knowledge for practitioners, and measured EYPS as equivalent to QTS rather than vice versa, continues to suggest the privileging of an education-driven agenda in this change. Teachers were not required to retrain or up-skill in their understanding of the learning and development needs of the youngest learners, but practitioners were.

The educational remit of the sector continues to be restated, challenging a professional role and identity located strongly in a discourse of child-centred care and substitute parenting. More recent government concern over children's school readiness, evidenced in the findings of the Bold Beginnings report (Ofsted, 2017), the reintroduction of the highly contested Baseline assessment and annual reports into the numbers of children achieving a 'Good Level of Development' (DfE, 2020, p. 6) continues to demonstrate the power of external authorities to change the identity of the early years practitioner. Since 2013, government has defined qualified staff as educators and teachers (DfE, 2013), as though caring element of the practitioner role is a matter of disposition, which can be left in the hands of the unqualified and less knowledgeable. It has been noted (Roberts-Holmes and Bradbury, 2016) that increasing attention has been paid to quantitative data as a means of measuring the quality of practice. Current EYFS and early learning goal reform has the potential to further influence early years practice and thus the role and identity of the practitioner, by privileging the assessment of literacy and mathematics in the EYFS Profile, and by foregrounding the learning needs of the Key Stage 1 child (DfE, 2020, p. 6).

Accommodating such change across the field of early years provision required changes to the roles and identities practitioners accepted for themselves. Where individuals lack the power to resist such change, the powerful will prevail, and proposed new ways of working or being are gradually subsumed within habitus. Hardy (2012) identifies this transition as a form of hysteresis, where the powerful set the structures to be accepted and over time, the less powerful comply and those who resist the transition must leave the field. Bourdieu (Bourdieu and Wacquant, 1992) uses the metaphor of an orchestra to explain this, where the composer and the conductor have the power to determine how each player will perform their individual part, and those whose contributions do not meet standards or expectations are written out of the piece. It is a rare and extremely powerful player who has the opportunity to contribute their own interpretation to the overall performance.

Fanciful though this metaphor might appear, it presents a vivid picture of where power lies within a changing field and how it is exercised. Work from Australia (Cook et al., 2013), where the early years sector has experienced similar change to its curriculum and regulatory framework, reported a concern amongst practitioners, especially child-minders, that an educational discourse was now overtaking their work, overshadowing the ethic of care and child-led practice that had initially drawn them into the sector. The response from those unhappy with this development was to leave. Similarly, the lack of a graduate mandate within the English regulatory framework for early years practice, and the continued inadequacy of government funding for nursery education places, have been deplored by those working in the early years sector. Meg, working in a private nursery chain, makes the point that to be able to lead practice higher levels of knowledge and a clear hierarchy is required:

> Management definitely need to be graduates …there's no point having a member of staff that is a graduate and a manager that is not and doesn't know what is relevant and what isn't.
>
> (Meg)

Penny, working in a private pre-school, also raises the issue of differential levels of funding between school and pre-school provision and what this says about government perceptions of the importance of the needs of the pre-school child:

> The pupil premium [in primary schools] is £1300 per child and going up, so we will be getting the early years' premium which is £300, so to me it shouts volumes as to how much they value what we do in the early years. It works out at about 53p an hour.
>
> (Penny)

However, rather than such awareness mobilising changes to the infrastructure of the sector, there has been a reduction in the number of graduate practitioners (NDNA, 2019), and the closure of settings that have become financially unsustainable.

The early years practitioner might reasonably be considered as a key actor within their field, being situated closest to the learning and developmental needs of the children they work with, and the wishes of their parents/carers. They are positioned to feel the greatest impact of change to this field imposed through political and social agenda. However, the ongoing workforce reform agenda for the early years sector, including new opportunities for professional education and training and new requirements for qualifications and registration, is set by government (DfES, 2006; DfE, 2017; DfE, 2021) and monitored through external inspection. As such, it represents a 'from above' (Evetts, 2011) approach to professionalisation, rather than 'from within', and clearly identifies where the power to determine the nature of this field and its relationships lies. Whilst the current approach to workforce reforms appears to raise career prospects and social capital for practitioners through access to higher education and graduate status, the lack of national infrastructure for career development and lack of mandate for graduate employment mean that significant career development can happen only when graduates leave the PVI sector and move to the compulsory education sector as qualified teachers. It also offers cover for a creeping managerial oversight from government of private provision and its staffing and practice, through statutory regulatory frameworks and inspection regimes. This apparent professionalisation is then less empowering and more compelling that it might at first appear.

The limitations this oversight places on the professional autonomy of the practitioner are then perpetuated by the restricted social and cultural capital of practitioners that has shaped their response to it. Their compliance with change driven by external authorities, and their acceptance of the authority of the powerful elites to drive such change demonstrates how power shapes the agency, practice and disposition of the individual. Their habitus is developed and sustained by social and cultural perceptions of their role and of those who choose to take it on, the pedagogy of their initial training and further professional development, and the willingness and capacity of the individual to question or challenge this, forming an alternative vision of what they consider their role to be. Colley et al. (2003) argue that roles and identity do not exist in a causal relationship, the one governing the other as the embodiments of field and habitus respectively. Rather, they co-exist in a relationship of mutual influence, and a vocational habitus (Colley et al., 2003) is developed.

The demands from field for a specific role to be fulfilled (in this case, from policymakers and regulators, rather than the workforce itself) will impact the identity of those individuals who take on that role (early years practitioners and teachers). Those with the power to demand a role, it could be argued, will also be those with the power to determine what that role will be, setting the jurisdictions and defining the vacancy (Abbott, 1988) it will fill. The identity of those fulfilling that role may influence its development and evolution, but this remains subject to the power they hold to wield such influence. Since the demand for early years practitioners has most recently been articulated by government, in order to meet their social policy agenda (DfEE, 1998; DfE, 2013), the power of the workforce to determine their identity, in Bourdieu's analysis, will be limited. By accepting the authority of government, the early years sector (both owners and practitioners) have positioned themselves as subordinate to standards of practice they have had limited say in establishing, further perpetuating a vocational habitus where compliance with authority remains central to the identity of the early years practitioner.

An ecological understanding of the early years sector

Bronfenbrenner's ecological model of development (Bronfenbrenner, 1986) presents human development as an 'evolving interaction' (Bronfenbrenner, 1979, p. 3), a dynamic process, subject to change driven by interaction between the individual and his/her environment, and shaped by individuals' perceptions of and responses to their environment. This would imply that the development of identity is a matter of individual agency and perception as well as a matter of power and capital. To understand the development of the individual, therefore, it is necessary first to understand how they perceive, understand and respond to their environment. However, although Bronfenbrenner appears to credit the individual with more agency in determining their identity through their social interactions, it should be remembered that opportunities for interactions may be governed and influenced by the social capital and confidence of the individual. Bourdieu's contention, that we form the closest relationships with those we spend most time with (Bourdieu, 1998), is for the early years practitioner perhaps one of the strongest factors in explaining how they articulate and understand their professional identity.

Bronfenbrenner's five systems within the environment impact the individual and their development, either through direct interaction between that system and the individual, or by indirect interaction, by means of social, cultural, political or historical influence. His emphasis on the immediate environment of the individual in shaping the development of their identity raises the issue of the lack of national infrastructure for the early years workforce and the fact that 80% of their sector comprises small organisations under private, voluntary or independent management and ownership. There are no nationally agreed roles or hierarchies beyond the mandated minimum requirements for qualified staff, and no nationally agreed descriptors or sets of responsibilities for practitioner beyond setting the boundaries of where Early Years Educators and Teachers can (and more specifically, cannot) be employed. Dalli, Miller and Urban (2012, cited in Miller, Dalli and Urban, 2012) argue that the role of the early years practitioner is 'embedded in *local* contexts, visible in relational interactions, ethical and political in nature, and involving multiple layers of knowledge, judgement and influences from the broader societal influences' (in Miller et al., 2012, p. 6, my italics). This constructs professional identity within a locally governed practice environment, perpetuating a vocational habitus appropriate to a specific organisation, one whose concerns include compliance with regulatory authority, and a neoliberal understanding of the parent as customer, to maintain its operation. These local contexts are further situated within a change agenda that includes responding to shifting political demands and economic pressures, new regulatory frameworks and entry qualifications, and changing perceptions of the purpose of early years provision and the needs of its key stakeholders. The understanding of identity then becomes a matter of critically evaluating how the individual and the organisation respond to such change – Bourdieu's concept of hysteresis – and if this change can be accommodated within a practitioner's existing values and behaviour, or if it can be resisted. To understand how environmental systems impact the development of the early years sector, Dalli et al. (2012) propose the use and adaptation of Bronfenbrenner's ecological model of development (Bronfenbrenner, 1986):

- Micro system: practice is understood as a series of relationships between practitioners, colleagues, children and families;
- Meso system: this is set within the context of team working, parent partnership, multi-agency working and key person working;
- Exo system: this is further surrounded by structures including the Local Authority, relevant legislation, funding for provision, the EYFS, inspections and quality assurance, registration requirements, parental employment and income, and accountability for practice;
- Macro system: this includes discourse on the purpose of early years provision, the role of the parent/carer, the social and cultural construction of the child, and social, economic and educational policy;

- Chrono system: this considers the influence of State involvement in education, the rights and needs of children, the social and political construction of the working mother, State involvement in family life, State involvement in the early years sector and the growing perception of the child as investment for the future.

The current role of the practitioner has developed through their relationships with their colleagues, employers and service users, within a context of recent organisational and sector-wide expectations of team working, inter-agency cooperation and a close personal relationship with the individual child. Figure 3.1 shows how this is situated within the development of political strategy to ensure sufficiency, sustainability and quality of provision, and the preparation of children for formal education. The inward pointing arrows indicate how policy to reduce welfare spending, a reconstruction of the role of parents in taking financial responsibility their families and the promotion of early intervention to address children's needs have all brought pressure to bear on the role and identity of the practitioner. Figure 3.1 also demonstrates the perception that although early years practice has a clear social, political and historical context, the prime concern for practitioners is the relationships and the day-to-day working with families rather than engagement on their part with the frameworks and authorities that regulate it.

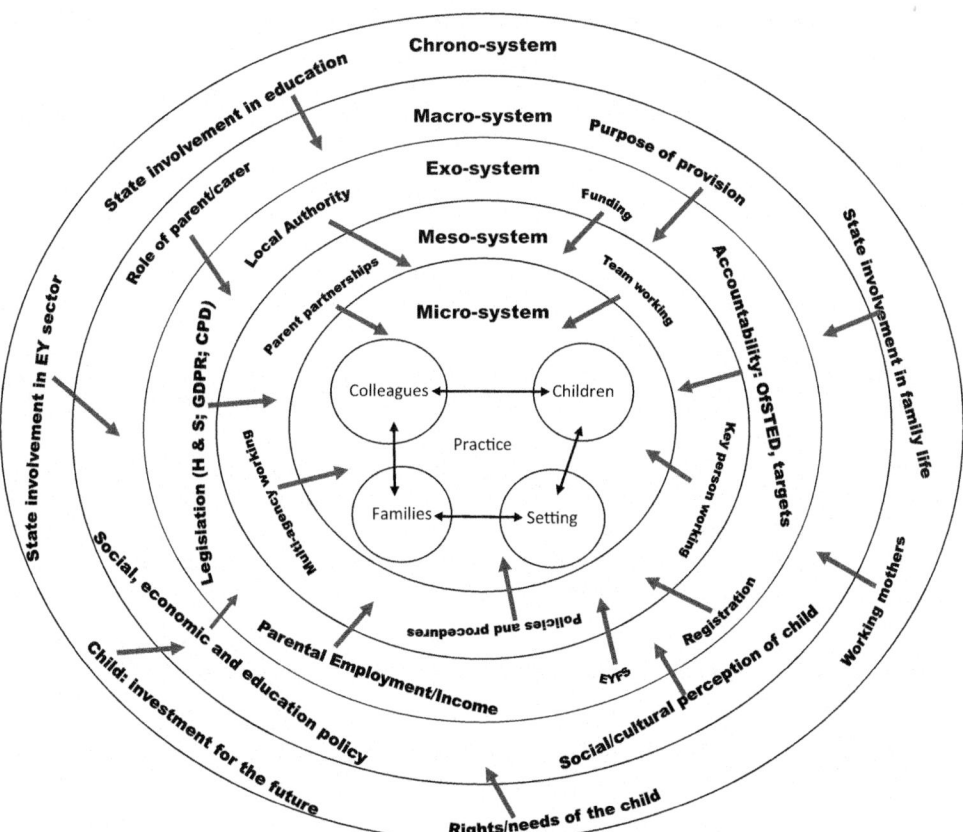

Figure 3.1 An ecological model of the development of early years practice and the role of the practitioner.

(Adapted from Dalli et al., 2012, p. 7)

Bronfenbrenner's model suggests that it is practitioners' immediate relationships within their social and cultural environment, their initial vocational education, their employment and their ongoing professional development that shape their sense of identity. Their perceptions of their role and purpose (Bronfenbrenner, 1979, p. 4), and how they chose to apply these to their own behaviour, make a significant contribution to this understanding, and are in turn mediated through how they are prepared for and supported in this role. The pedagogic approach to the vocational training and CPD of the early years practitioner shapes their understanding of their role as much as its content and level. A strongly technical/rational approach (Schon, 1983), based on the demonstration of practical competence, constructs their role as a series of steps to be applied in order to ensure a pre-determined outcome. Restricting the initial vocational training of the practitioner to such an approach at a relatively low level of achievement (NVQ levels 2, 3) encourages a perception of good practice as determined by trainers rather than personal judgement or in response to the unique developmental needs of an individual child. Unless encouraged to engage in critical reflection, practitioners then construct themselves as needing to remember and apply received wisdom, rather than contributing through their own experience to the knowledge base of their organisation and their sector.

Bronfenbrenner (1979, 1986) also argues that environment alone is not enough to shape the development of the individual, but that this is also the product of their engagement with their environment, beyond passive or unconscious acceptance and compliance. Such a framework implies a level of personal agency and responsibility for identity, based on the interactions and perceptions of the individual. Therefore, practitioners' response to change in their less immediate environments will also influence their development of identity and their understanding of their role. However, this engagement is mediated through their vocational training, ongoing CPD and opportunities for professional socialisation (Lumsden, 2012) across the wider workforce, most particularly through the vocational habitus these experiences establish. A vocational habitus that privileges disposition and relationships over higher academic qualifications or a sense of professional self as a critical creator of knowledge through research will encourage an identity based on the day-to-day elements of practice and the immediate satisfaction of service users, managers and inspectors. Such emphasis may not only present the practitioner with a socially approved and generally recognised way of framing their identity, but it may also actively discourage them from challenging this established doxa or developing an alternative identity. The composition of the environment for the early years practitioner is therefore a strong controlling force in the development of their identity, very much the structuring structure that Bourdieu argues frames habitus and the balance of power within a field.

Tensions in the professional identity of the early years practitioner

The professional identity of the early years practitioner is a complex, multifaceted construct, crossing boundaries of care, education and well-being, which can be problematic when establishing the specialism of the practitioner and the unique expertise they bring to their role. Research in Australia (Berthelsen and Brownlee, 2007; Brownlee et al., 2000) has identified that early years practitioners describe their role in unsophisticated language, emphasising their caring, rather than educational, role, which has the potential to undermine the specialist knowledge they apply to their work. Moss (2006) cautioned against presenting early years practice as a matter of care rather than education, arguing that such a potentially dispositional and gendered account of practice undermined its status. Sims-Schouten and Strittrich-Lyons (2013) describe how practitioners in the English ECE workforce continue to separate their professional identity into a practical and an academic self, so that doing is understood as being distinct from knowing, and practical skills from intellectual abilities. This makes determining the status of the practitioner problematic, particularly within the education community, due in some part to the gendered and classed nature of the workforce, and its levels of qualification. When this is coupled with an historical and cultural perception of early years provision as providing safe supervision and substitute parenting, care rather than education, then the vocabulary and discourse of early years practice plays a significant role in shaping how its workforce is perceived by others and understands itself.

However, professional identity is also a personal as well as an official construction, and tension between the two can give a clearer indication of the level of agency exercised by individual practitioners in the undertaking of their practice. Practitioner agency in determining effective practice and a sense of professionalism rests on whether or not the regulatory framework is perceived as a document for interpretation, or a document for compliance, raising the question of the power of practitioners in this self-determination. By questioning what practitioners consider to be good practice when working with young children, and what they use as a context for reflecting on its quality (Dyer, 2018; Dyer and Taylor, 2012), it emerges that early years practitioners recognise the value of universal educational outcomes in charting progress in children's learning, and the place of such a framework in identifying children's learning needs, and external judgements of the quality of their provision. However, they return to a more relational and affective construction of their identity, citing children's social and emotional needs, children's rights to play and to respect, and the underpinning principles of the EYFS when asked what they consider good practice to be. Rose, working in a classroom support role for young children in a primary school, explains her own sense of practice values very strongly:

> Children need nurture, they need attachments, they need understanding, they need empathy … my personal, most important thing is my relationships with the children … good practice [is] seeing that a child is an individual child instead of a uniform in a group.
>
> (Rose)

But despite her articulation almost of a manifesto for practice based on the needs of the child, her overriding concern with her job is that it may corrupt her sense of values, and it causes her distress when she has to work with colleagues who do not share her views. Either she does not see it as her role to change colleagues' perceptions or organisation practice or policy, or she lacks the agency to engage with those elements of her environment that would enable her to do so.

Conclusion

Since the role of the early years practitioner has most recently been shaped and repurposed by government, and their practice increasingly governed by externally set regulatory and inspection frameworks, this suggests their identity is the product of their responses to this influence. Even today, the identity of the early years practitioner is most often constructed in terms of their dispositions and values rather than through functionalist criteria about specialist knowledge or autonomy over practice standards and qualifications, or the purpose of their role (Dyer, 2018). This perception is embedded in the practitioner and perpetuated through a vocational education that characterises good practice as a series of processes and procedures, a particular disposition towards children and compliance with practice standards. The value placed on the development of an appropriate disposition and compliance with regulatory authorities appears to emphasise the subordinate role of the practitioner in meeting the needs and requirements of others – children, parents, employers, regulators. This, in turn, is compounded by the traditional recruitment to this workforce of young, working-class women, with limited academic qualifications (Skeggs, 1988), and therefore limited social and cultural capital through which to claim agency and self-determination over their professional identity and practice standards. These factors, along with a dominant discourse of practice developed by those who fund and licence practice, contribute to a form of pedagogic violence (Bourdieu and Passeron, 1990), a structuring of education to meet the hegemonic demands of a powerful elite that not only transmits a knowledge base but also controls how individuals both see and present themselves. Such violence will only be addressed through changing the overall pedagogy of professional education. Professionalisation of a workforce cannot only be achieved through an investment in human capital – the up-skilling of individual practitioners (Hargreaves and Fullan, 2012) through the acquisition of prescribed skills and knowledge. It also requires the workforce to develop decisional capital in building its own knowledge base and applying its own judgement on good and appropriate practice. These two elements should then be supported by the development of an infrastructure for career development (McGillivray, 2008) including a mandatory hierarchy of qualifications.

The theoretical frameworks discussed here all indicate that professional identity is a self-constructed and also socially constructed concept. Therefore, both the workplace and the academic classroom represent valuable contexts for developing a sense of self for the individual practitioner, along with an awareness of their professional values and confidence in their own agency. Closer examination of leadership culture and the pedagogy of professional education, over the next three chapters, identifies how these factors have contributed to the current role and status of the early years practitioner, and how they can be used to support the development of decisional and social capital required (Hargreaves and Fullan, 2012) for the professionalisation of a workforce to be advanced.

References

Abbott, A. (1988). *The System of Professions: An Essay on the Division of Expert Labour*. London: University of Chicago Press Ltd.

Berthelsen, D. and Brownlee, J. (2007). Working with toddlers in child care: Practitioners' beliefs about their role. *Early Childhood Research Quarterly*, 22, 347–362.

Bourdieu, P. (1977). *Outline of a Theory of Practice*. Cambridge: Cambridge University Press.

Bourdieu, P. (1998). *Practical Reason: On the Theory of Action*. Cambridge: Polity Press.

Bourdieu, P. and Passeron, J.-C. (1990). *Reproduction, Education, Society and Culture* (2nd ed.). London: Sage.

Bourdieu, P. and Wacquant, L. J. D. (1992). *An Invitation to Reflexive Sociology*. London: University of Chicago Press Ltd.

Bronfenbrenner, U. (1979). *The Ecology of Human Development: Experiments by Nature and Design*. Cambridge, MA: Harvard University Press.

Bronfenbrenner, U. (1986). Ecology of the family as a context for human development. *Developmental Psychology*, 22 (6), 723–742.

Brownlee, J., Berthelsen, D., Boulton-Lewis, G. and McCrindle, A. (2000). Caregivers beliefs about practice in infant childcare programmes. *International Journal of Early Years Education*, 8 (2), 155–165.

Burr, V. (2015). *Social Constructionism* (3rd ed.). East Sussex: Routledge.

Colley, H. (2006). Learning to labour with feeling: Class, gender and emotions in childcare education and training. *Contemporary Issues in Early Childhood*, 7 (1), 15–29.

Colley, H., James, D., Dimont, K. and Tedder, M. (2003). Learning as becoming in vocational education and training: Class, gender and the role of vocational habitus. *Journal of Vocational Education and Training*, 55 (4), 471–498.

Cook, K., Davis, E., Williamson, L., Harrison, L. J. and Sims, M. (2013). Discourses of love in family day care. *Contemporary Issues in Early Childhood*, 14 (2), 112–126.

Dalli, C., Miller, L. and Urban, M. (2012). Early childhood grows up: Towards a critical ecology of the profession. In Miller, L., Dalli, C. and Urban, M. (eds.), *Early Childhood Grows Up: Towards a Critical Ecology of the Profession*, 3–19. London: Springer.

Department for Education and Employment (DfEE) (1998). *The National Childcare Strategy: Meeting the Childcare Challenge*. London: HMSO.

DfE (2013). *More Great Childcare: Raising Quality and Giving Parents More Choice*. Crown Copyright.

DfE (2017). *Early Years Workforce Strategy*. London: DfE.

DfE (2020). Early years foundation stage profile: 2021 handbook (EYFS reforms early adopter version June 2021). Crown Copyright: 2020.

DfE (2021). *Statutory framework for the early years foundation stage*. Crown copyright.

DfES (2005). *Children's Workforce Strategy, Consultation Paper*. London: DfES.

DfES (2006). *Children's Workforce Strategy: Building a World Class Workforce for Children, Young People and Families. The Government Response to the Consultation*. Nottingham: DfES Publications.

Dyer, M. and Taylor, S. (2012). Supporting professional identity in undergraduate Early Years students through reflective practice. *Reflective Practice: International and Multidisciplinary Perspectives*. https://doi.org/10.1080/14623943.2012.670620

Dyer, M. A. (2018). Being a professional or practising professionally. *European Early Childhood Education Research Journal*, 26 (3), 347–361.

Evetts, J. (2011). A new professionalism? Challenges and opportunities. *Current Sociology*, 59 (4), 406–422.

Foucault, M. (1982). *The subject and power*. In Dreyfus, H. and Rabinow, P. (eds.), *Michel Foucault: Beyond Structuralism and Hermeneutics*. Chicago: University of Chicago Press.

Hardy, C. (2012). Hysteresis. In Grenfell, M. (ed.), *Pierre Bourdieu: Key Concepts* (2nd ed.). Durham: Acumen.

Hargreaves, A. and Fullan, M. (2012). *Professional Capital: Transforming Teaching in Every School*. London: Routledge.

Hordern, J. (2016). Knowledge, practice and the shaping of early years professionalism. *European Early Childhood and Education Research Journal*, 42 (4), 505–520.

Kay, L., Wood, E., Nuttall, J. and Henderson, L. (2021). Problematising policies for workforce reform in early childhood education: A rhetorical analysis of England's Early Years Teacher Status. *Journal of Education Policy*, 36 (2), 179–195. https://doi.org/10.1080/02680939.2019.1637546

Lumsden, E. (2012). *Early Years Professional Status: A New Professional or a Missed Opportunity*. Doctoral Thesis. The University of Northampton.

McGillivray, G. (2008). Nannies, nursery nurses and early years professionals: Constructions of professional identity in the early years workforce in England. *European Early Childhood Education Research Journal*, 16 (2), 242–254.

Miller, L., Dalli, C. and Urban, M. (eds.). (2012). *Early Childhood Grows Up: Towards a Critical Ecology of the Profession*. London: Springer.

Moss, P. (2006). Structure, understandings and discourses: Possibilities for re-envisioning the early childhood worker. *Contemporary Issues in Early Childhood*, 7 (1), 30–41.

National Day Nurseries Association (NDNA) (2019). NDNA 2018/19 Workforce Survey England. Huddersfield: 2019.

Nutbrown, C. (2012). *Foundations for Quality: The Independent Review of Early Education and Childcare Qualifications Final Report*. London: Crown Copyright.

Ofsted (2017). *Bold Beginnings: The Reception Curriculum in a Selection of Good and Outstanding Primary Schools*. Manchester: Ofsted.

Rabinow, P. (ed.). (1984). *The Foucault Reader: An Introduction to Foucault's Thought*. London: Penguin.

Roberts-Holmes, G. and Bradbury, A. (2016). The datafication of early years education and its impact upon pedagogy. *Improving Schools*, 19 (2), 119–128. https://doi.org/10.1177/1365480216651519

Schon, D. (1983). *The Reflective Practitioner: How Professionals Think in Action*. Aldershot: Ashgate Publishing.

Sims-Schouten, W. and Strittrich-Lyons, H. (2013). 'Talking the talk': Practical and academic self-concepts of early years practitioners in England. *Journal of Vocational Education and Training*, 66 (1), 39–55.

Skeggs, B. (1988). Gender reproduction and further education: Domestic apprenticeships. *British Journal of Sociology of Education*, 9 (2), 131–149.

Chapter 4

Leadership and professionalisation

Introduction

This chapter presents an overview of a range of models and approaches to leadership in ECEC and draws on doctoral research to consider how organisational culture influences the way the graduate practitioner leads. It also introduces some of the emerging reconceptualisations of leadership and highlights the unique features of the sector which shape the practice of leading in ECEC. The chapter begins by focusing on the link between leadership and professionalisation and considering the complexities of leading in ECEC.

Leadership and professionalisation in ECEC in the PVI sector have become integrated through successive agendas to up-skill the workforce and improve quality of provision (Fairchild, 2019) as exemplified with the introduction of Early Years Professional Status (EYPS) in 2006, whereby the Early Years Professional (EYP) was identified as a 'change agent' (CWDC, 2006, p. 4) tasked with improving and leading practice. Although EYPS was replaced by Early Years Teacher Status in 2013 and the commitment to have a graduate leader in every PVI setting by 2015 was reversed, as Palaiologou and Male (2019) point out, government policies demand skilful leaders and highly qualified professional staff even though the sector consistently features low status and low levels of pay. This is an emblematic tension of a quasi-free market model of provision, where private businesses are heavily reliant on inadequate government funding whilst being subject to high levels of centralised control and accountability (Penn, 2019). This tension matters because leadership does not occur in a vacuum; it is influenced by social, cultural, political and economic factors at the macro and micro levels. Leadership in ECEC is complex and situated; therefore, it is important for leaders to be able to analyse, evaluate and reflect on their practice using theory and research.

In presenting a selection of models it can suggest that in settings only one model may be in operation at one time; this is rarely the case. Also, particularly in small settings, management and leadership are often used interchangeably in practice (Aubrey et al., 2012). Management is often understood as focusing on day-to-day tasks which are essential in ensuring safe and sustainable provision, but they can divert time away from leading pedagogy and practice (Aubrey et al., 2012). Furthermore, the introduction of graduate-level professional qualifications has failed, according to Palaiologou and Male (2019), to address the challenge in the sector to identify a point of accountability which differs from that of the leader/manager, who has areas of responsibility far beyond pedagogy. Palaiologou and Male (2019) suggest that it is not useful to try and import

DOI: 10.4324/9780367815387-4

models of leadership into the sector and call for a reconceptualisation of leadership that is the responsibility of the whole workforce, and is based on relationships and collaboration. Arguably this reconceptualisation is aspirational as it is predicated on a consistent, qualified and motivated workforce which does not align with the current profile of the ECEC sector in England which has high rates of staff turnover, difficulty recruiting appropriately qualified practitioners, falling numbers of practitioners studying for higher levels of qualification and lacks opportunities for training and development (Bonetti, 2019). Therefore, in presenting a range of different models of leadership the intention is to facilitate a reflective, reflexive, flexible approach suited to an evolving context rather than promote a single model of best practice. Here the focus is on leading pedagogy and practice.

Models of leadership

Distributed leadership

Distributed leadership refers to a model of shared responsibility defined in terms of influence rather than authority; it is common organisational practice in schools, universities and some PVI settings. This model is sometimes described as democratic as it reflects a vision of leadership which is more collaborative and inclusive, and Lockwood (2016) suggests it makes leadership more accessible to the individual practitioner, particularly if they are reluctant to lead. Deeply embedded gender stereotypes have traditionally cast men as leaders and women as supporters and nurturers, which is potentially problematic in a sector which is overwhelmingly female. Hallet (2014) argues that distributed models of leadership facilitate women moving to the forefront of leading provision. In addition, such a participative approach builds leadership capacity and sustainability, develops skills and potential, and offers opportunities for career enhancement and professional development. Despite the advantages of this model of leadership some owners and managers of settings can be reluctant to delegate responsibility; this is perhaps unsurprising when the workforce is characterised by low levels of qualification, high staff turnover and lack of access to training (Bonetti, 2019). Furthermore, Palaiologou and Male (2019) highlight that the point of accountability resides with the owner/manager of the setting despite the fact that others may have a leadership role. A distributed model of leadership signals a move away from the traditional idea of an individual leader holding all the power towards a relational and communal model where all can be a leader and engage in leadership (Siraj and Hallet, 2014). This understanding of leadership fits with the idea of a pedagogical leader as identified by Nutbrown (2012) who suggests all practitioners, regardless of qualification, should be capable of demonstrating pedagogical leadership.

Pedagogical leadership

Dalli (2008) argues that ideas from professionalisation in ECEC in New Zealand have influenced professionalisation in England, and this extends to ideas about the role of the professional as a leader of practice. In New Zealand, the Education Reform Office (ERO) (2015) reported on quality in early childhood services and on reviewing leadership concluded that

High quality services have leaders who are inspirational, enthusiastic and innovative thinkers. These leaders manage change effectively, motivate others to make change and have a good awareness of pacing change that leads to improved quality.

(p. 6)

The report also goes on to acknowledge that the emerging discourse in early childhood in New Zealand focuses on pedagogical leadership, where the focus is on high-quality teaching and learning and it involves 'change conversations' (p. 17) within the workplace. ERO (2012) identifies four overarching principles of pedagogical leadership, and the key assumption of these principles is the 'change agent' or continuous improvement dimensions of the work.

The four overarching implementation principles of pedagogical leadership identified by ERO (2012, p. 17) are that it:

- has staff with credibility and expertise
- is ethical, creative, strategic and focused on improvement
- uses effective professional learning and development processes
- should be part of an effective set of networks.

In many PVI settings operating in a competitive business context financial and day-to-day staffing concerns are likely to be a leadership priority (Penn, 2019) and therefore, arguably, at odds with establishing organisational conditions where these principles operate. This could put pedagogical leadership out of reach of the individual practitioner. Therefore, practitioners might find it helpful to understand the pedagogical leader as a change agent as discussed in a range of international literature including Roberts-Holmes (2013), in England, Cecchin (2009), in Denmark and Coughlin and Baird (2013) in Ontario. However, Douglass (2019), in a review of international approaches to leadership and quality in ECEC, found that managing change requires specific skills and that pedagogical leaders often had insufficient time to dedicate to quality improvement, as they spent at least one third of their time ensuring compliance with policy and regulatory frameworks. Whilst there is often tension between the core functions of pedagogical and administrative leadership, pedagogical leaders value the role highly (Douglass, 2019). Pedagogical leadership is central to effective teaching and learning and includes supporting staff development, creating trusting relationships with and among staff and extending into the community, facilitating peer learning and promoting implementation of the curriculum and assessment (Douglass, 2019).

Furthermore, Siraj and Hallet (2014) describe pedagogy as where education and care meet and that the pedagogical leader is concerned with creating conditions in which members of the organisation can give their best in teaching and learning to support the holistic development of the child. They argue that pedagogical leadership is activated by 'passion' (Siraj and Hallet, 2014, p. 113) where passion is a strong emotional enthusiasm, a deep and sound commitment for working with young children (Hallet, 2014). For the aspiring pedagogical leader it might be helpful to reflect on their passion and to keep in mind Coughlin and Baird's (2013) description of pedagogical leaders as individuals who see themselves as 'partners, facilitators, observers and co-learners' (p. 1). With these descriptions of the pedagogical leader their influence on practice does not rely on their position in the leadership structure of the setting, which resonates with the Catalytic Model of leadership envisioned by McDowall Clark (2012).

Catalytic leadership

In this model McDowall Clark (2012) describe a leader who sees the possibility for change through a supportive, non-confrontational, reflective process where they use influence to bring about small incremental changes; in short the leader is a catalyst for change. Change emerges through the process of reflection and is therefore democratic rather than imposed from above. Whilst such a participative model might emphasise stereotypically feminised leadership traits, build on an ethic of care and so be popular with practitioners (Hard and Jonsdottir, 2013; Siraj and Hallet, 2014), it might also be slow in bringing about important improvements in practice. This model has much in common with the models for distributed and pedagogical leadership in that it is participative and democratic.

Effective leadership in ECEC

There is debate about the most effective type of leadership in ECEC. Heikka and Waniganayake (2011) argue that leadership in ECEC combines pedagogical leadership and distributed forms of leadership. They suggest that early childhood leaders are responsible for creating a community that fosters learning and communication. This resonates with Oberhuemer's (2005) idea of participative or democratic professionalism, which seeks to empower through co-construction of learning. Hadfield et al. (2012) describes a model of practice leadership emerging from the bottom up and is differentiated from organisational leadership. This model recognises that improvement activities are bounded by wider structural issues which the practice leader may or may not be able to influence (Hadfield et al., 2012). Practice leadership is limited, but it is also potentially enhanced by structural factors such as staff ratios, levels of staff qualifications, funding for equipment and working conditions. Ultimately in this model of practice leadership the focus is on aspects of practice the leader can influence regardless of position in the organisation. Siraj and Hallet (2014) acknowledge that leadership in ECEC is evolving and argue that effective leadership for learning must be collegial, relational, reflective, nurturing and caring. Palaiologou and Male (2019) argue for leadership in ECEC as pedagogical praxis which eschews imported models of leadership and embraces the peculiarities of ECEC bringing together a continual interplay between theory, actions and practice, praxis. They argue for pedagogical leadership which is rooted in its context and environment extending out onto the community, and able to defend ECEC values in light of policy reforms.

Leadership and power

All of the models included here reconceptualise leadership as collaborative, democratic and emphasise the use of influence rather than the exercise of power by the leader. However, yet to be resolved is the key debate in respect of the extent to which a formal position of power and authority is required to implement change. The attitude to and the exercise of power in leadership in ECEC is complex. Hard and Jonsdottir (2013) describe the highly feminised nature of the workforce as creating a workplace culture within a 'discourse of niceness' (p. 319). 'Niceness' is entwined with the expectation and ethic of care which then prevails into an expectation of intra-staff behaviours. Hard and Jonsdottir (2013) found in their study that the 'discourse of niceness' led to problems of leadership enactment. An attempt to be collaborative stifled difference, leading to conformity and a lack of discussion about difference in order to avoid conflict. Paradoxically, this led to behaviours which they describe as 'horizontal violence' (p. 317), defined as 'psychological harassment' which can include verbal abuse, humiliation, excessive criticism, exclusion and denial of access to opportunity, as well as discouragement, disinterest and withholding of information. This is in stark contrast to the 'discourse of niceness' but demonstrates frustration in the workforce with the avoidance of debate and open discussion around leadership and power (Hard and Jonsdottir, 2013). In addition, conformity in leadership and practice is likely to stifle change and improvements to pedagogy and practice.

Leadership of pedagogy and practice in ECEC is complex, and Fairchild (2019) suggests that the sector has a confused understanding of the role of leader conflated with notions of professionalisation, professional status and management and shaped by wider political agendas. There are problems adopting and adapting leadership models in a diverse range of settings, but Bolman and Deal (2017) suggest that successful leadership can be facilitated through understanding how organisations work so that the leadership role can fit the setting, rather than through a one-size-fits-all approach.

Understanding how organisations work

Bolman and Deal (2017) suggest that we carry mental models or frames in our head, that is, a set of ideas and assumptions which help us understand a particular territory, in this instance the organisation. They further suggest that it is necessary to use multiple frames, to re-frame and seek alternative perspectives to gain a better understanding of an organisation. They have identified four frames from the literature on leadership in organisations; these are the structural, human resource, political and symbolic frame and they are explained in the following section.

The structural frame

The structural frame depicts a rational world and treats an organisation as a factory (Bolman and Deal, 2017). This frame emphasises organisational architecture, including how the organisation allocates responsibilities, and the rules, policies, systems and hierarchies created to coordinate the activities of the organisation. One of the central assumptions underpinning the structural frame is that, if formal roles and responsibilities are suitably allocated, peoples' performance will be maximised. Bolman and Deal (2017) assert that problems occur when organisational structure does not fit well with current circumstances and suggest that in every organisation the structure must evolve to fit the circumstances. Bolman and Deal (2017) state that a team structure emphasising hierarchy and top-down control works well for simple, stable tasks, but during times of change the structure of the organisation must also change to develop lateral forms of communication and coordination. Bolman and Deal (2017) point out that flexible structures can improve participation and quality and in ECEC would make room for the pedagogical leader.

The human resource frame

Bolman and Deal (2017) state that the human resource frame views the organisation as an extended family where the needs of the individual and the goals of the organisation align. However, individuals and groups within an organisation have different needs and will often compete for power and resources which can cause conflict. Underfunding of the PVI sector means that tension exists between quality of provision and profit, potentially undermining the goals of the individual practitioner and the setting to provide high-quality ECEC. Through the lens of the human resource frame, we are reminded that money is a powerful incentive, but people want things that go 'beyond money' (p. 120) from their work. Bolman and Deal (2017) suggest that viewed through the human resource frame the key challenge is for organisations to find ways for individuals with all their limitations to get the job done, whilst feeling good about themselves. There are a range of motivational strategies which can be implemented to strengthen the bond between the individual and the organisation such as job security, paying well and training. Other strategies seek to empower staff through participation, job enrichment and egalitarianism. for example. through models of distributed leadership but, as Bolman and Deal (2017) point out, 'broader, more egalitarian sharing of power is resisted worldwide' (p. 150). Furthermore, they suggest that managerial skills and understanding can be in short supply. and when managers are unable to handle the social, economic and practical elements of change, they revert to self-protection. For the leader of pedagogy and practice to succeed when the manager feels vulnerable, they will require political skills such as bargaining, negotiation and compromise; this leads into the political frame.

The political frame

Rather than viewing the organisation as a family, the political frame, as outlined by Bolman and Deal (2017), views the organisation as a jungle and is concerned with organisational politics, conflict, coalitions and power. For a sector with such a gendered workforce, which is imbued with and dependent upon the cultural stereotypes of women as caring and nurturing, there may be some reluctance to apply this frame. It is in fact this reluctance to consider ECEC settings through this frame which can lead to problems, as identified by Hard and Jonsdottir (2013). Agreement is easier to achieve when everyone shares the same values, beliefs and cultural ways but at every level of human affairs often they only partly overlap. Within the political frame, power is the most important asset and power can be defined as 'the potential ability to influence behaviour, to change the course of events, to overcome resistance, and to get people to do things they would not otherwise do' (Bolman and Deal, 2017, p. 186).

Bolman and Deal (2017) explain that conflict over scarce resources is at the heart of day-to-day dynamics in the political frame. They argue that conflict is not necessarily problematic; it can stimulate creativity and new ideas but, if there is too much or it is poorly managed, then it can lead to in-fighting and destructive power struggles. Bolman and Deal (2017) suggest that, whilst 'efforts to eliminate politics are futile' (p. 203), it is possible to develop skills as a political leader they suggest that, at the start, an effective leader must set an agenda, that is, outline a goal or vision, and a strategy for achieving the goal. The key political skill in setting the goal and outlining the strategy is sensitivity; that is, the leader knows how others think and the agenda responds to their concerns. The effective leader should also develop a political map which means they anticipate potential challenges and identify individuals who are likely to resist change. Bolman and Deal (2017) also write that the key to getting things done is through relationships; it is important to have friends and allies and equally important to foster informal communication with potential opponents. Such a relational approach is congruent with leadership in ECEC whereby, for example, the pedagogical leader may need to bargain and negotiate in order to make changes. Bolman and Deal (2017) suggests that the leader should adopt an approach of conditional openness. This approach starts with open and collaborative behaviour and maintains this approach unless the individual is adversarial. Then the leader responds accordingly and remains adversarial until the opponent makes a collaborative approach. The leader should ensure that this is carefully managed to avoid political differences leading to conflict which could impact negatively on children, their families and other members of staff. The idea of the leader in ECEC deliberately taking an adversarial stance is arguably controversial and thus missing from the models of leadership associated with the sector. However, Bolman and Deal (2017) argue, like it or not, leaders and managers face ambiguity and scarcity and need to make tough decisions daily, but if their adversarial stance is friendly and forgiving, and based on passion, persistence and diplomacy, it can be effective. In ECEC the leader should draw on their ethic of care and be comfortable that their actions are in the best interests and feelings of others.

The symbolic frame

Bolman and Deal (2017) suggest that the symbolic frame, unlike the other frames, sees organisational life as serendipitous and the symbolic frame tempers 'the assumptions of rationality prominent in other frames' (p. 18). The symbolic frame views organisations as cultures driven by rituals, symbols, stories, heroes and myths (Bolman and Deal, 2017). The individuals working in the organisation are actors who must play their parts appropriately; otherwise, problems may arise; rituals and symbols lose their meaning (Bolman and Deal, 2017). Myths, vision and values imbue the organisation with purpose. There are competing tensions in the PVI sector, for example, between quality and profit, but Siraj and Hallet (2014) remind the leader that the vision must focus on pedagogy as the purpose is to provide education and care which supports the holistic development of the child. Caring for young children has great significance for practitioners in ECEC but, as moral leaders, caring extends to concern for the needs of the workforce, which starts with listening and understanding. Bolman and Deal (2017, p. 392) also describe caring as the 'ethical glue' which holds an organisation together, and this relates to the view of moral leadership from the symbolic frame.

The research study

The doctoral research study (McMahon, 2016) which is referred to in this chapter explored the experiences and perspectives of four experienced practitioners – Laura, Debbie, Emma and Karen – as they undertook a programme of training and education to become EYPs. A narrative approach was taken to the collection, interpretation and presentation of the data. There were three layers of data analysis, and this chapter focuses on the third layer which drew on the multiframe model of Bolman and Deal which offers insight into how organisational structures and practices shape participants' experiences of becoming an EYP and their ability to lead practice and bring about change (Tables 4.1 and 4.2).

Ideas from each frame can help the practice leader identify the barriers to change which occur in their setting and highlight some of the essential strategies to use to overcome these barriers.

Table 4.1 The Multiframe Model of Barriers to Change with Essential Strategies

FRAME	BARRIERS TO CHANGE	STUDY FINDINGS	ESSENTIAL STRATEGIES	EXAMPLES FROM NARRATIVES
Human resource	Staff feelings of anxiety, uncertainty and incompetence Being needy	Effective leaders developed political skills of negotiation, agenda setting and building alliances to bring about change.	Training to develop new skills Participation and involvement of staff Psychological support for staff	Emma trained her staff Karen asked her colleagues for ideas and feedback Lauren was mentored by her manager
Structural	Loss of direction, clarity and stability for staff Confusion and chaos in the setting	Graduate professional challenged the traditional organisational structures in the setting.	Communication between the leader and all colleagues Realigning and renegotiating formal patterns and policies in the setting	Debbie confronted the management team Emma devolved some of her management tasks
Political	Disempowerment for staff Conflict between winners and losers	Effective leaders developed political skills of negotiation, agenda setting and building alliances to bring about change. Effective leadership was built on moral leadership which supported and protected the workforce.	Developing arenas where issues can be renegotiated and new coalitions formed	Lauren negotiated and discussed changes with staff in placement Karen built alliances with parents Emma protected her staff from the adverse effects of changes to policy through agenda setting and negotiation
Symbolic	Loss of meaning and purpose for staff Staff clinging to the past	Effective leaders identified the symbolic forms which bind individuals to the organisation and endeavour to match the motivational needs of the employee to the needs of the organisation	Creating transition rituals for staff Mourning the past Celebrating the future with all stakeholders	Symbolic forms can be interpreted negatively as suggested in Karen's narrative or motivational needs neglected; as a result individuals may leave the setting. Positive examples included; Emma discussed telling parents about EYPS in a newsletter or on a notice board-this could be a transition ritual or a way to celebrate success. Debbie shared her ideas for practice in her new setting and felt respected and valued by her employer.

The four frames: Essential strategies

Human resource

When viewed through the human resource frame, the participants' narratives suggest that individuals in an organisation, including managers, as reported by Karen and Debbie, can fear practical, social and economic elements of change. Government policy is a powerful and, since 1997, a frequent lever for change in the PVI sector. Small settings, managing scarce resources, are more vulnerable than large organisations to the possible adverse effects of changes brought about through government policy, as suggested in Emma's narrative. Relevant to such contexts Siraj and Hallet (2014) acknowledge that the challenge for the practice leader in ECEC is to lead the process of change in a participatory way. Even when change is experienced as for the good, people do not like to feel voiceless, and, if they are asked to do something they do not understand, they can feel incompetent and powerless (Bolman and Deal, 2017). Therefore, the first key strategy is that the practice leader of an ECEC setting takes time to hear people's ideas and concerns and to make sure that all concerned have the knowledge and expertise to carry out their responsibilities. For example, Lauren referred to being mentored by her aunt as important to her in developing her expertise, while Emma also identified mentoring as something she used to support and develop the expertise of the staff in her setting. Mentoring has the potential to be particularly effective in a small PVI setting where it can be implemented quickly as the practice leader is likely to be familiar with the staff and their responsibilities, thus reducing the amount of time when individuals feel incompetent and powerless. Siraj and Hallet (2014) acknowledge that members of an organisation want transparency in change processes where leaders explain the reasons for change. Therefore, a second strategy, which can be employed by the practice leader in ECEC and demonstrated by Emma, is to take time to explain new initiatives to the staff in the setting, as, for example, when Emma provided training on sustained shared thinking.

Structural frame

One of the key findings from the multiframe analysis of the narratives suggests that the introduction of the graduate professional into the setting challenged the traditional organisational structures, and this was particularly problematic where the graduate was more highly qualified than the manager. Therefore, this is likely to be challenging for any new practice leader as their introduction into an ECEC setting might be perceived as undermining existing structural arrangements in the setting. In the short term, the practice leader may not be in a position to change the structural arrangements in the setting, but they may be able to rework them informally. This strategy was employed by Lauren, who highlighted the need to build relationships with the other staff in her placement setting. She explained, 'you want to be a leader but don't want to come across as taking over'. As Bolman and Deal (2017) suggest, to informally realign structures requires effective communication to build alliances and coalitions. Similarly, Rodd (2013) agrees that communication is a fundamental aspect of effective leadership in ECEC. In the PVI sector, if the manager continues to feel undermined by the practice leader it may be necessary for the practice leader to build alliances and coalitions outside the setting as suggested in Karen's narrative. Karen turned to parents for support, and in ECEC in the PVI sector parents are important stakeholders and can be powerful allies for the practice leader.

However, in seeking to build alliances and coalitions, the practice leader should proceed cautiously to avoid undermining and alienating individuals, and they need to be open to the possibility of horizontal violence (Hard and Jonsdottir, 2013). As Siraj and Hallet (2014) point out there will inevitably be some resistance to change, so the leader must be confident in managing conflict and be sensitive in handling people involved in the change. Over time, the practice leader may be able to negotiate more formal changes to the structural arrangements; this will depend on their ability to build relationships with their colleagues in the setting and their ability to influence those with authority such as the management team.

Political frame

From the perspective of Bolman and Deal's (2017) political frame, it is important for the practice leader to recognise that change invariably generates conflict. Bolman and Deal (2017) explain that conflict arises because some members of the organisation may oppose, some sit on the fence and some support the change; this can lead to clashes. This was evident in the stories of the participants. For example, Debbie explained that a clash with her management team, which she described as 'a little blow out', led to a positive outcome for her. Whilst 'a little blow out' can be helpful, sometimes clashes smoulder under the surface, and Bolman and Deal (2017) suggest that coercive power, rather than legitimate authority, determines who wins. In this scenario, the would-be change agent often loses. Bolman and Deal (2017) recommend that the best way to manage conflict in organisations is through negotiation, and Hallet (2014) supports this argument asserting that professional dialogue underpinned by the values of ECEC and a vision to improve and shape practice can reduce conflict. Looking at ECEC settings specifically, the practice leader might do this by establishing regular meetings or forums to talk, listen and negotiate. Siraj and Hallet (2014) agree, arguing that in this way employees feel consulted and have an opportunity to have their questions answered. Emma implemented this strategy she said, 'we have meetings with an agenda now', and, when the setting was threatened with closure, Emma talked openly to the staff and they then had a better understanding of the challenges faced by Emma in trying to keep the setting open. However, the practice leader must remember that issues are unlikely to be resolved instantly; they are often ongoing and, as the organisation is dynamic, issues will change. If clashes do erupt the practice leader must be able to confront the conflict and to do this they may need support from established coalitions, and from the management team.

Symbolic frame

Viewing the participants' narratives through the symbolic frame led to the key finding that effective leaders identify the symbolic forms which bind an individual to the organisation and endeavour to match the motivational needs of the individual to the needs of the organisation. This matters in the PVI sector because, as the participants' narratives suggest, when this frame is neglected then individuals may look for a job in another setting where their needs are more closely aligned to those of the organisation. When an experienced, qualified individual leaves the setting it can adversely affect the quality and consistency of care and recruiting a suitable replacement can be costly. Bolman and Deal (2017) point out that systems, policies, routines, rituals and even how a setting is laid out can all take on symbolic value, and changes to these can result in people feeling a sense of loss. Regular meetings, informal and formal, can provide space to talk, and even griping can be part of the ritual (Bolman and Deal, 2017); however, the practice leader also needs to encourage letting go of the old ways, and this can be done by celebrating success. There are practical steps that the practice leader in ECEC can take to celebrate success; one strategy, suggested by Karen, was to display qualifications on the wall and Emma considered telling parents about staff achievements in a newsletter.

Bolman and Deal (2017) explain that the effective leader needs to think about symbols on a deep level above all creating 'symbolic glue' (p. 417) so the team is a cohesive group pulling together for a common purpose. They can do this through words and examples, influencing positively colleagues in the setting as both Emma and Karen identified in their narratives. Siraj and Hallet (2014) point out that the attitude a change leader adopts influences how others view the change process; therefore, it is important for the practice leader to be a positive role model. Hallet (2014) argues that the leader should draw on their passion and enthusiasm to keep staff motivated and committed to change. Many women work in ECEC because they have a deep emotional commitment, 'passion' (Hallet, p. 18), for ECEC and care deeply for and about young children. Therefore, the practice leader in ECEC has a unique opportunity to unify the workforce in the setting behind this shared value. The findings suggest that the practice leader can do this through moral leadership whereby they support and protect the workforce rather than exploit their ethic of care. Emma provided examples of protecting the workforce in her account, and Lauren described the support she received from the manager in her setting. Emma's position as the owner and manager of the setting allowed her the authority to ensure her employees were not exploited; however, not all practice leaders will be in a position of authority like Emma; therefore, moral leadership might be exemplified by Karen who overcame considerable challenges to lead and change practice, and in the process inspired one colleague to apply to become an EYT. Hallet (2014) argues that passion underpins a leadership style which is nurturing, caring, inclusive and influencing rather than authoritarian; however, this study suggests that it can be difficult to disentangle moral leadership, in the PVI sector, from authority.

A multiframe approach offers a chance to get beyond stereotypical and oversimplified views of leadership, and this is important in ECEC where, nuanced and sensitive leadership is required to reflect the unique features of ECEC in the PVI sector. The practice leader in ECEC must exert influence to bring about change and from the outset they need to understand the barriers to bringing about change in an organisation.

Tabular representation is set out in Table 4.1 (p. 54) of the barriers a leader in ECEC might face when bringing about change in an organisation. There are four rows drawn from Bolman and Deal's multiframe model (2017): human resource, structural, political and symbolic frame. The corresponding columns are barriers to change, study findings, essential strategies and examples from the narratives. The table is designed to support the leader in anticipating potential barriers to change and how they might be overcome.

Barriers to change and practice leadership

By understanding organisational life through the four frames the practice leader has the opportunity to reflect and adapt to their context; they also have the opportunity to anticipate some of the challenges they may face in trying to bring about changes to practice. All leaders need the cooperation and collaboration of others (Baldoni, 2010). Hadfield et al. (2012), suggest that individuals in a setting are the biggest barrier to implementing improvement strategies. The practice leader can only bring about change in their setting if the people are prepared to change and can deal with their own emotional response to change. Siraj and Hallet (2014) argue that to lead change the leader must understand the process of change and how individuals and groups in the setting might feel about, and respond to change. The Change Curve Model (Kubler-Ross, 1989) encapsulates effectively the stages of change in a model which is readily applicable and accessible to the practice leader in ECEC. It was initially developed to explain the stages of grief in terminal patients; however, Chapman (2013) notes that, during times of change in organisations, individuals will often react in the same way as people experiencing grief (Figure 4.1).

Stage 1 Shock and Denial: This refers to individuals feeling that everything was fine as it was, without understanding why it has to change, and in stage one individuals are shocked and react with denial which is a buffer, giving the individual time to collect themselves, usually as a temporary defence.

Stage 2 Frustration and Depression: This might be recognised when individuals become anxious and angry and their performance in an organisation dips. This stage might lead to a period of conflict in the setting.

Stage 3 Experiment and Decision: This can be understood as the stage when individuals accept that change is inevitable; they try to work out what their role will be and begin to work with the changes.

Stage 4 Integration and Acceptance: The final phase refers to a time when the individuals have fully accepted the change and it becomes a reality.

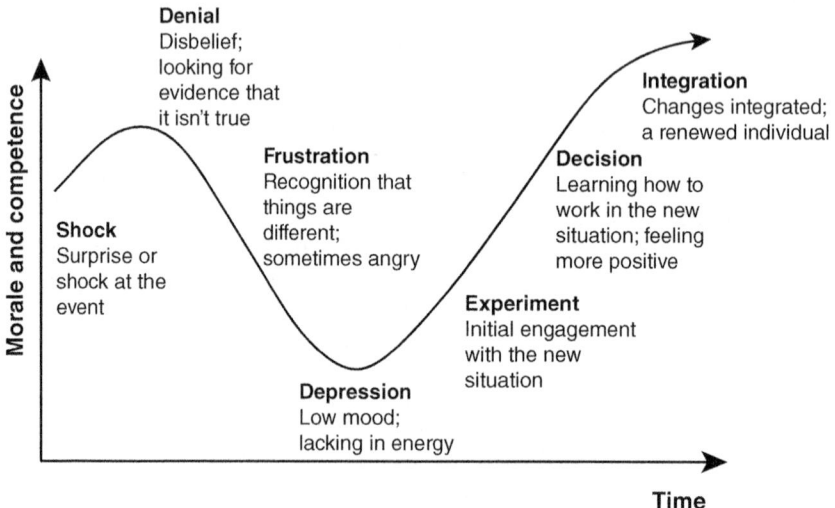

Figure 4.1 The Change Curve Model.

(Adapted from Kubler-Ross, 1989)

A new model for practice leaders

In the following section the two models, Bolman and Deal's multiframe model (2017) and the Change Curve Model (Kubler-Ross, 1989), have been combined and contextualised to practice leadership in ECEC by drawing on examples from my research. The purpose of this combined model is to equip the practice leader with the skills to identify barriers to change at the organisational and individual levels, and equip them with strategies to exert influence to bring about change. It is necessary because, as Siraj and Hallet (2014) point out, change can produce uncertainty and confusion in people and the practice leader must identify ways to help them overcome these feelings, and move towards embracing new ways of doing things.

It supports the leader in understanding the barriers to change which arise from the organisational structure, and from individuals within the organisation. Bolman and Deal's (2017) four frames – structural, human resource, political and symbolic – represent the organisational structures and the four columns of the table, and Kubler-Ross's Change Curve (1989) is used to organise the four rows of the table, shock/denial, frustration/depression, experiment/decision, and integration, to reflect the individual's experiences. Table 4.2 includes examples of strategies used by graduate professionals from the author's research to equip the leader for practice.

Table 4.2 The Change Curve Four Frame Model of Leadership

Change Curve Model: stages of change	Structural frame	Human resource frame	Political frame	Symbolic frame
Shock and Denial	Identify what the existing structures are. Reflect and Identify what changes may be needed.	Communicate little and often. Engage in reflective dialogue Allow time to adapt. Avoid overwhelming individuals.	Network with colleagues and stakeholders. Build coalitions	Tell a compelling story to colleagues and stakeholders. Co-create a vision. Communicate this vision to colleagues and stakeholders, for example parents, governing body and external professionals.
Frustration and Depression	Create structures to support the process. Identify who does what and when.	Hold meetings with colleagues and stakeholders, encourage collaborative reflections and gather feedback.	Build alliances with colleagues and stakeholders. Diffuse opposition, and confront conflict	Be a visible leader. Continue to communicate the vision to colleagues and stakeholders. Continue to reflect on practice and provision.

(Continued)

Table 4.2 (Continued)

Change Curve Model: stages of change	Structural frame	Human resource frame	Political frame	Symbolic frame
Experiment and Decision	Alter structures that do not support change. Plan for short term successes	Provide training for colleagues. Hold meetings and get feedback. Engage in collaborative reflection. Build involvement with colleagues and stakeholders.	Empower individuals. Continue to build alliances with colleagues and stakeholders.	Communicate progress and celebrate success. Create new symbols and rituals which colleagues can share.
Integration and Acceptance	Align the operational structure to the new culture	Continue to build broad involvement. Communicate and get feedback from colleagues and stakeholders.		Communicate progress, celebrate success. Share stories of the journey and continue to develop the new culture, continue to reflect.

Conclusion

This chapter has provided an overview of some common models of leadership found in ECEC including distributed and pedagogical. It also considered reconceptualised approaches to leadership which rely on influence rather than authority. Together these provide insight into the range of approaches in operation in the sector. However, these models do not fully acknowledge the unique features of the PVI sector and the challenges that a graduate practice leader might face. Therefore, the chapter then draws on empirical doctoral research to consider how organisational culture and the way individuals react to change affect practice leadership. From this research the chapter introduces a new model, the Change Curve Four Frame Model of Leadership, which extends understanding of practice leadership in ECEC bringing together practical strategies and theory to reflect organisational reality in the PVI sector. The model is underpinned by a desire to collaborate and influence through effective communication. It relies on moral leadership built upon an ethic of care which includes children, families and staff. As such, this model incorporates and reflects many elements of the reconceptualised models of leadership discussed in this chapter and speaks to the evolving nature of practice leadership in ECEC. The following chapter continues to draw on data from the doctoral thesis to further develop the idea of reconceptualising by applying it to models of professionalism, and it extends the exploration of leadership in ECEC by considering how it connects to new models of professionalism emerging in the sector.

References

Aubrey, C. et al. (2012). How do they manage? An investigation of early childhood leadership. *Educational Management Administration and Leadership*, 41 (1), 5–29.

Baldoni, J. (2010). What does the organization need me to do? *The Journal for Quality and Participation*, 33(1), 10.

Bolman, L. and Deal, T. (2017). *Reframing Organisations: Artistry, Choice and Leadership* (6th ed.). San Francisco: Jossey-Bass.

Bonetti, S. (2019). The early years workforce in England: A comparative analysis using the Labour Force Survey. Education Policy Institute and Nuffield Foundation.

Cecchin, D. (2009). *Pedagogical Institutions as Objects for Leadership*. EECERA Strasbourg 2009.

Chapman, C. (2013). Building the leadership capacity for school improvement. In Harris, Alma et al. (eds.) *Effective Leadership for School Improvement*, London: Routledge, 137–155.

Children's Workforce Development Council (CWDC) (2006). *Early Years Professional Prospectus*. Leeds: CWDC.

Children's Workforce Development Council (CWDC) (2008). *Guidance to the Standards for the Award of EYPS*. London: CWDC.

Children's Workforce Development Council (CWDC) (2010). *On the Right Track: Guidance to the Standards for the Award of Early Years Professional Status*. Leeds: CWDC [online] Last accessed 15/3/2022 http://webarchive.nationalarchives.gov.uk/20110908152055/http:/www.cwdcouncil.org.uk/eyps/standards

Coughlin, A. M. and Baird, L. (2013). *Pedagogical Leadership*. Ontario: Queen's Printer.

Dalli, C. (2008). Pedagogy, knowledge and collaboration: Towards a ground-up perspective on professionalism. *European Early Childhood Education Research Journal*, 16 (2),171–185.

Douglass, A. (2019). Leadership for Quality in Early Childhood Education and care: OECD Education working paper No. 211. [online] Last accessed 28/4/22 https://www.oecd.org/officialdocuments/publicdisplaydocumentpdf/?cote=EDU/WKP%282019%2919&docLanguage=En

Education Reform Office (ERO) NZ (2012). *Alternative Education: An evaluation of the Pedagogical Leadership initiative*. [online] Last accessed 15/3/2022 Alternative Education: Schools and Providers | Education Review Office (ero.govt.nz)

Education Reform Office (ERO) NZ (2015). *New Zealand Education System Overview*. [online] Last accessed 29 May 2016 at http://www.education.govt.nz/assets/Uploads/NZ-Education-System-Overview-publication-web-format.pdf

Fairchild, N. (2019). The micropolitics of posthuman early years leadership assemblages: Exploring more-than-human relationality. *Contemporary Issues in Early Childhood*, 20 (1), 53–64.

Hadfield, M. et al. (2012). *First National Survey of Practitioners with EYPS*. Walsall: CeDare and University of Wolverhampton.

Hallet, E. (2014). *Leadership of Learning in Early Years Practice*. London: Institute of Education, University of London.

Hard, L. and Jonsdottir, A. (2013). Leadership is not a dirty word: Exploring and embracing leadership in ECEC. *European Early Childhood Education Research Journal*, 21 (3), 311–326.

Heikka, J. and Waniganayake, M. (2011). Pedagogical leadership from a distributed perspective within the context of early childhood education. *International Journal of Leadership in Education*, 14 (4), 499–512.

Kubler-Ross, E. (1989). *On Death and Dying*. London: Routledge.

Lockwood, S. (2016). "Leadership" In L. Trodd (ed.) *The Early Years Handbook for Students and Practitioners: An Essential Guide for the Foundation Degree and Levels 4 and 5*, pp. 433–447. Abingdon: Routledge.

McDowall Clark, R. (2012). 'I've never thought of myself as a leader but…': The Early Years Professional and Catalytic Leadership. *European Early Childhood Education Research Journal*, 20 (3), 391–401.

McMahon, S. (2016). *Early Years Professional Status: A narrative study of leadership and contradictory professionalism*. Doctorate in Education, Sheffield Hallam University available at British Library EThOS: https://ethos.bl.uk/OrderDetails.do?uin=uk.bl.ethos.700580

Nutbrown, C. (2012). *Foundations for Quality: The Independent Review of Early Education and Child Care Qualifications*. London: Crown Publications. [online] Last accessed 15/3/2022 https://www.education.gov.uk/publications/eOrderingDownload/Foundations%20for%20quality%20-%20Nutbrown%20final%20report.pdf

Oberheumer, P. (2005). Conceptualising the Early Childhood Pedagogue: Policy approaches and issues of professionalism. *European Early Childhood Education Research Journal*, 13 (1), 5–16.

Palaiologou, I. and Male, T. (2019). Leadership in early childhood education: The case for pedagogical praxis. *Contemporary Issues in Early Childhood*, 20 (1), 23–34.

Payler, J. and Locke, R. (2013). Disrupting communities of practice? How 'reluctant' practitioners view early years workforce reform in England. *European Early Childhood Education Research Journal*, 21 (1), 125–138.

Penn, H. (2019). Understanding the contexts of leadership debates. *Contemporary Issues in Early Childhood*, 20 (1), 104–109.

Roberts-Holmes, G. (2013). The English Early Years Professional Status (EYPS) and the split Early Childhood Education and Care (ECEC) system. *European Early Childhood Education Research Journal*, 21 (3), 339–353.

Rodd, J. (2013). *Leadership in Early Childhood: The Pathway to Professionalism* (3rd ed.). Maidenhead: Open University Press.

Siraj, I. and Hallet, E. (2014). *Effective and Caring Leadership in the Early Years*. London: Sage.

Siraj-Blatchford, I. and Manni, L. (2006). *Effective Leadership in the Early Years Sector*. London: The Institute of Education University of London.

Chapter 5

Reconceptualising professionalism in ECEC

Introduction

This chapter explores contemporary debates on professionalism in ECEC drawing on critical views of the professional from beyond the sector which argue that the imposition of externally imposed measures of productivity is exploitative and contradictory to notions of professionalism. This chapter includes practitioner's narratives from doctoral research to illustrate how abstract debates and notions of professionalism are experienced by practitioners. It examines new models of professionalism emerging in the sector in England and internationally and considers the links between professionalism, policy and quality. The chapter goes on to explore the connection between models of professionalism and leadership in ECEC identifying the relational aspects of both whilst acknowledging that leadership which fails to question policy and practice might be at odds with the model of a critically reflective professional. It then draws on the work of Bourdieu to explore how gender and class influence professionalisation. To conclude the chapter recognises that a model of professionalism is emerging which is democratic and relational in nature and requires critical reflection on policy and practice if necessary. However, the conclusion acknowledges that low pay in the sector remains a significant impediment to professionalisation and professional recognition.

Critical views of the professional

Crook (2008, p. 10) provides a useful historical perspective on professionalism. He reminds us that such terms as 'profession', 'professional' and 'professionalism' are contested terms and change over time. Therefore, it can be difficult to provide one definition. Crook (2008) describes the distinguishing characteristic of a professional as having 'an intellectual technique acquired by special training' (p. 16). He argues that a profession can exist only where there is a bond between the practitioners and that this bond must take the shape of a formal association. Crook (2008) does point to other traits which have been associated with a profession including: systematic preparation with a taught, intellectual component and observation of norms or codes of practice; an emphasis on service to others ahead of personal reward and high levels of personal integrity. Whitty (2008) writes about the 'shifting phenomenon of professionalism' (p. 28), stating that previously the most established professions such as law and medicine enjoyed 'licensed autonomy' (p. 28). However increasingly, even for these professions, professional status is now determined by the state through employment and regulation,

DOI: 10.4324/9780367815387-5

and this brings high levels of accountability and control. A range of authors including Schon (1992), Ritzer (2001), and Ball (2003, 2008) raise the issue of government control as part of this discourse of the demise of the professions.

The literature which discusses the demise of the professions provides further insight into the contested nature of professionalism. Schon (1992), in his seminal paper, describes a crisis in confidence with and amongst professionals. He points to the fact that the public have demanded increasing external regulation of professional practice, therefore bringing into question the professions' privileged social position and autonomy. This mode of external regulation measures the performance, output and productivity of the individual which Ball (2003) identified as performativity. He blames performativity for reducing the professional to technician, and Ball (2008) discusses the effect of performance management systems on the 'subjectivities of individuals' (p. 51); he states, 'performativity invites us and incites us to make ourselves more effective, to work on ourselves and to feel guilty and inadequate if we do not' (p. 51). Furthermore, he points out that performativity is enacted through externally imposed measures and targets, against which the professional must position them self. These targets offer the possibility of being better, better than others or even the best. Ball (2008) posits that this creates uncertainty for the professional and is a tactic for destabilisation of the workforce, and that performativity is most powerful 'when it is inside our heads and our souls' and 'when our moral sense of ourselves and our desires are aligned with performativity' (p. 52). This can lead to individuals feeling that they can never meet external requirements, and that practice is never good enough. Ball (2008) describes performativity as leading to 'ontological insecurity' (p. 54), whereby professionals lose sight of what is important in what they do and call into question the meaning in what they do. Performativity can deflect attention away from the personal, social and emotional activities which underpin the relationships between children and practitioners and have no immediate performative value (Ball, 2008); this was illustrated in a quote from Debbie's narrative:

> It's hard, really hard with the workload I'm juggling and I bring a lot of work home from work, with planning, phonics and the data; I do everything the nursery teacher does but I'm supposed to be with the children thirty four hours, but sometimes when I'm with the kids my heads everywhere else and that's upsetting. Then with an impending Ofsted due, all the paperwork has to be up to date. You've caught me on a bad day, too much to do, too little time. I'm on track in my head but not on paper; everything I'm doing for work links in to it (EYPS), all I need to do is to track it, to remember that, and put it to the front of my mind.

However, the findings suggested that the 'ontological insecurity' experienced by my participants was temporary and they welcomed the improved status, they perceived, that state regulation implies. This aligns with Oberheumer's (2005) suggestion that professional standards and qualifications bring professional recognition and status. As Karen explained, 'I do want a title and that status; I think the title is important for self-esteem and how people view you'. Hadfield et al. (2012) found that the graduate practitioners in their study gained increased feelings of confidence from having the status and in my research Karen, Lauren and Debbie stated that having a degree was important particularly for its cultural and symbolic value in society, as Debbie said, 'For people outside the setting the degree is important, it's going up in the world'.

New models of professionalism in ECEC

The participants in the study struggled, at times, to balance meeting the children's needs with meeting the plethora of external performance measures and targets. Nevertheless, their commitment to working with young children remained strong and at the heart of their practice. This correlates with models of professionalism which have an 'ethic of care and emotional labour' (Osgood, 2006b, p. 193) at their core, including Manning-Morton (2006) and Osgood (2006b, 2010) who are keen to define a new professional who is characterised by the intensely personal and emotional nature of early childhood education and care.

Rodd (1998: 2013) and Oberheumer (2005), call for a new democratic professional in ECEC. This may be inevitable as Barnett (2008) points out that it is impossible for professionals to hold onto their epistemological authority as in the knowledge society everyone is knowledgeable to some extent. The democratic professional also espouses values and practice associated with the 'social pedagogue' model (Stephens, 2009, p. 343). He proposes that the defining feature of best social pedagogic practice is the 'capacity to become a secure adult base in a child's life' (p. 345). He borrows the term 'secure base' from Bowlby and his theory of attachment, and stresses that the emphasis is on human relationships based on openness and equality, as opposed to supervision and hierarchy, seen as a feature of practice in England. Stephens (2009) states that there is a connectedness between the teacher and learner, where the affiliation is expressive rather than instrumental, and at odds with a system of ECEC that relies on external measurement. In Stephens' model of the professional pedagogue the bond between the child and the teacher is more than what can be conveyed through actions, it is emotional and full of feeling. There is much agreement with these assertions in the writing of Elfer (2007, 2008, 2010) and Manning-Morton (2006), who describe the fundamental importance of relationships and attachment in ECEC practice in England. Elfer (2007 p. 186) also acknowledges that 'working professionally with young children is an intensely personal undertaking'.

Page (2017, 2018) further develops the idea of a model of professionalism in ECEC which draws on attachment theory, and Nodding's (1984) ethic of care to conceptualise professional love as a reciprocal relationship, complementary to that of parent and child, but emotionally intensive which drives effective practice. Page (2018, p. 135) presents a model of Professional Love which is intended to support the practitioner to develop their own principles, policies and practice, a 'pedagogy of love' (p. 136) which the professional can draw on in daily practice. This model is important because it reflects the intensely complex nature of providing effective education and care for young children, which Page (2018, p. 137) argues is 'debunked' in policy and arguably is marginalised by a focus on children's cognitive outcomes in the operationalising of professionalism in ECEC.

Unfortunately models of professionalism which draw on attachment theory and place relationships and professional love at their core leave the workforce open to exploitation (Taggart, 2011). This exploitation is evident when considering levels of pay in the ECEC sector. Bonetti (2019) found that the childcare workforce earns on average five pounds an hour less than the average female population and in real terms has suffered a 5% pay reduction since 2013, compared to a 2.5% increase for all working women. This matters as pay is a visible indicator of the low status of the sector and the workforce, and reflects the low value placed on a model of professionalism built on an individual ethic of care.

Policy and Professionalism

Taggart (2011) drew attention to the potential for exploitation when practitioners base their professionalism on an individual ethic of care which expects individual practitioners to shoulder a moral burden of educating and caring for children on behalf of society. He argues for a move from an individual to 'political ethic of care' (p. 86) which shifts the moral burden to the heart of society and social justice. However, this shift is challenging for practitioners and society, society because it is likely to be costly to the taxpayer or parents and to practitioners because their identity is deeply embedded in the vocational nature of the work (Payler and Locke, 2013). The shift is further complicated by the subordinate position of women in ECEC by virtue of their gender and class. Furthermore, professional identity and models of professionalism are shaped by policy discourse and from the outset EYPs were constructed in contradictory ways, as the saviours of society and as presiding over a failing sector (Osgood, 2009). In addition, the sector had no control over the body of knowledge or the pace of change which defined their professionalism making them dependent on policy for validation of the model of professionalism (Hordern, 2013). Government interest in professionalisation, as articulated through Labour's policy to have a graduate level practitioner in every setting, has waned, signalled as far back as 2012 when this requirement was removed from the revised EYFS. Then in 2017 the DfE retracted proposals in the workforce strategy to grow the graduate workforce in poorer areas and decided against allowing EYPs and EYTs to lead maintained nursery classes (Ceeda, 2019). In the same report Ceeda identified that by doing this the DfE has taken away a coherent career structure for graduate practitioners and failed to address inequalities across allied professional fields. When considered alongside the low levels of pay it is unsurprising that enrolment on EYTS courses has fallen so that there were only 365 new entrants in 2018–2019. Furthermore, settings are reporting that government funding is inadequate so they must cut costs and or charge parents additional fees, and one way they cut costs is by lowering their qualification mix (Ceeda, 2019).

Nevertheless, the workforce remains integral to the success of government policy, and they are positioned in policy as instrumental in ensuring children have the best possible start in life and are reminded in the introduction to EYFS (DfE, 2021) that the experiences children have in the early years have a major impact on their future life. They are central to government policy to improve social mobility and reduce the attainment gap between the least and most disadvantaged whereby all three- and four-year-olds are entitled to up to 30 hours free education, and the most disadvantaged two-year-olds to 15 hours. In 2009 Osgood argued that the ECEC workforce held a key position in government policy as the means by which the government can achieve its vision for an economically successful nation, and the amelioration of many societal ills, and this is still the case.

International concepts of professionalism in ECEC

It is not just in England that a complex and evolving policy framework influences the development of ECEC. Campbell-Barr et al. (2015) point out that across the globe there is increased interest and investment in ECEC. Increasingly international governments recognise the value of early education and care in supporting children's development and also in supporting parental employment. Vrinioti (2013) draws our attention to the Bologna Process in 1999 as the catalyst to improving the education of early childhood workers across Europe. This trend follows the common and widely accepted assumption that pre-school education is the basis for lifelong learning and that pre-school education, as highlighted in the PISA Study of 2001, had failed to instil positive attitudes to learning in the 15-year-old students surveyed (Vrinioti, 2013). Therefore, in order to improve the pre-school system, priority was placed on improving the education of early childhood workers, and this is an ongoing process in many countries at the current time (Campbell-Barr, Georgeson, and Selbie 2015).

In the United States, for example, Arndt et al. (2018) suggest professionalism is defined in limited credential college-degree-based ways within a plethora of quality ratings for provision, and in Australia raising the level of qualification is at the core of professional identity in the sector. Similarly, in Ireland the focus is on raising the level of qualifications of the workforce, and they are increasingly overburdened with improving quality and accountability measures. Arndt et al. (2018) argue that globally forces of uniformity, standardisation and pre-determined outcomes are disproportionately shaping ECEC services and professionalism, even in Denmark which has traditionally taken a very different approach. The Danish pedagogue was understood to be a facilitator of children's learning, embedded within a democratic and non-hierarchical management system. However, during the 1990s intensification of state regulation and the introduction of a curriculum and testing of young children led to a more instrumental model of professionalism. Whilst it can be argued that this has improved the professional reputation of the pedagogue, Arndt et al. (2018) highlight that it has led to a split in practice whereby documentation and reality of practice are different.

Professional subjectivities in ECEC are shaped by local and global forces, and there are some commonalities such as increasing credentialism, and accountability measures whilst little attention is given to the poor working conditions, low pay and low status of the workforce. Campbell-Barr et al. (2015) also state there is increasing international recognition that quality of the service matters, but in many countries decisions about the skill set required for working in ECEC have become a top-down political process, embedded in increasingly bureaucratic procedures.

Professionalism and quality

Melhuish and Gardiner (2020) point out that extensive research (Sylva et al., 2010; Melhuish et al., 2015; Melhuish and Barnes, 2018) has shown that ECEC can have a positive effect on children's cognitive, behavioural and social outcomes particularly if it is of good quality. Good quality provision makes the greatest difference to the outcomes of the most disadvantaged children (Melhuish and Gardiner (2020)); therefore, any model of professionalism in ECEC must consider what is meant by quality.

The Education Policy Institute (EPI) reported in 2018 that despite considerable research and a projected government spend of £6bn on childcare provision in 2019/20 there is a lack of clarity into what high-quality provision looks like. Nevertheless, the EPI have set out two ways of looking at quality in ECEC (EPI, 2018, p. 5).

Structural quality: the focus is on easily observable inputs which are measurable and regulated including group size, child: teacher ratios, staff retention and teacher training and development.

Process quality: the focus is on the children's day to day experiences including educational activities, types of interactions between children, teachers and parents and the way in which routine care needs are met.

A large-scale longitudinal study of the quality of early years provision in England (Study of Early Education and Development by Melhuish and Gardiner SEED, 2018) focused on both structural and process elements to measure overall quality in one thousand settings including PVI, nursery schools and children's centres. Importantly the study suggests that improvements in quality in the last 16 years appear to be associated with concurrent improvements in staff qualifications and identified that the most common level of managers' qualification was Level 6. In addition, SEED emphasised the significance of practitioner–child interactions, specifically sustained shared thinking (SST). This research provides a powerful argument for graduate professionals who can engage in and promote SST. However, the compelling research evidence of the link between higher levels of staff qualifications and quality of practice and provision (Sylva et al., 2010; Melhuish and Gardiner, 2018) is largely ignored in in the early years statutory framework and as part of the quality inspection process undertaken by the Office for Standards in Education (Ofsted), as only the manager of a setting is required to have a Level 3 qualification (DfE, 2021). Ofsted use the following evaluation schedule to judge quality.

- Overall effectiveness
- The quality of education
- Behaviour and attitudes
- Personal development
- Leadership and management

(Ofsted, 2021)

Colmer (2017) argues for professionals who can, when necessary, challenge government policy and resist practice which is not developmentally appropriate or in the best interests of the child. She suggests that this requires a model of professionalism which emerges through collaboration and reflective conversations. Furthermore, Colmer (2017) found that professional identity was nurtured through collaborative professional learning whereby practitioners worked together to understand and critically reflect on government reform. Such reflection is integral to establishing quality practice which is child-centred. This is illustrated in Emma's narrative when she describes how working towards becoming a graduate practitioner helped her to focus on quality, not as set out by Ofsted but by focusing on the children and being a role model and leader to her staff. Emma said:

> The status, it's enabling me to focus on quality, not Ofsted 'outstanding' but about what is going on with the children. If I'm going to be a role model, I need to be able to do it myself and want it to be about developing all the staff. In some ways I didn't think I had the right. To be fair, they have much more experience than me, I tried to be manager and friend. I wasn't leading, I was coaching not even coaching. I was either doing it myself or thought I was modelling and expecting them to follow and they didn't. As an example, when I used to do an observation on staff, they didn't bat an eyelid because I just skirted round the issues. Now they say, 'Oh I haven't prepared anything'. I'm leading; it has created a role that wasn't there but needed to be there, it's clarified my role and the deputy is managing more. I was trying too hard to be everyone's friend, but I was also very controlling. I used to go through their daily diaries every night and we had an hour a week when I double checked the folders. We've moved away from how to do the assessment folder to how can I deal with this? Less task focused and managerial, more supervision.

In this excerpt from Emma's narrative working towards the graduate professional status was integral to her reflecting on her leadership style, and this correlates with current reconceptualisation's of professionalism in ECEC which are closely integrated with concepts of leadership in the sector.

Professionalism and leadership

As identified in Chapter 4 there were powerful policy drivers in England linking professional status with leadership particularly leading change to improve quality in ECEC. Whilst the EYP competency standards did not articulate a specific approach to leadership, in practice because many EYPs could not rely on a position of authority within an organisation they had to lead through influence. To effectively influence colleagues the graduate practitioner was required to mentor and support colleagues (Hadfield et al., 2012) and this was echoed in my own research. In addition, the doctoral research suggested that leadership based on influence often has to be nurtured and developed over time through a process of negotiation, collaboration and ultimately required strong mutually respectful relationships. Models of leadership including pedagogical, distributed and catalytic which break from reliance on authority and power emphasise the relational aspects of practice, as do democratic models of professionalism. A model of professionalism which is underpinned by relationships with children, families, colleagues and key stakeholders reflects the caring purpose at the heart of professional identity in ECEC and is closely allied with the new model of leadership proposed in my research, the Change Curve Four Frame Model of Leadership, and finds similarities with distributed and pedagogical models of leadership. Furthermore, Sims et al. (2015) points out that leadership consists of professional knowledge, professional identity, using an interpretive lens and developing relational trust. Therefore, leadership in ECEC and professional identity are intertwined and in process, subject to local and global policy, organisational culture and shaped by gender and class.

There are tensions with aligning relational models of leadership and professional identity as highlighted by Sims et al. (2015). Their research suggests that some leaders are so focused on the relationships as an outcome in themselves that they lose sight of their role in mentoring, coaching and supervision to improve practice. Furthermore, Sims et al. (2015) argue that the current models of leadership do not encourage leaders to challenge the dominant practice quality discourse as set out in top-down policy frameworks; rather, they focus on understanding policy better to implement it effectively. Leadership which does not challenge the dominant discourse may be at odds with the idea of a professional who goes beyond compliance with quality frameworks so that quality practice is determined from the bottom-up rather than top-down. In this way professionals generate new knowledge and new practice, and without this they are unlikely ever to be valued as a profession (Sims et al., 2015). However, Kay et al. (2021) point out that leaders in ECEC are required by policy to be leaders for social justice against a backdrop of wider economic priorities and daily are charged with being leaders of people, pedagogy and curriculum, quality and change, and unsurprisingly due to this complexity they struggle to enact their roles effectively. Kay et al. (2021) therefore argue that increasing policy demands on the ECEC workforce have highlighted the illusion of devolution through professionalisation versus the realities of surveillance and increasing responsibilities of leadership.

Gender, class and professionalism

Andrew (2015) states that the logic of professionalisation is that higher standards and better training will result in higher wages, but wages, in real terms, in England in the PVI sector have gone backwards since 2013 (Bonetti, 2019). This might be explained by understanding how the historical schemes in relation to social class and gender have impacted on the sector (Andrew, 2015). The work of Bourdieu (1992, 1977), particularly his ideas of capital and habitus, offers a possible explanation for why women, often working class, make up the majority of the workforce in ECEC. He suggests that through primary conditioning women identify themselves and are identified by society as caring, and working-class women use the available economic and cultural capital to work in ECEC. Thus, caring for children is seen as natural women's work and has little economic value. There is a long-standing divide between education and care in England, whereby childcare is associated with the PVI sector and education with schools and the maintained sector. This divide persists despite practitioners in both sectors delivering the same curriculum framework and being subject to the same regulatory and inspection framework. This divide extends to the workforces in education and care where unresolved classing issues continue to shape the field (Andrew, 2015). Bourdieu (1984) argues that traditionally professions have been dominated by those with access to significant amounts of capital, including educational capital, which until recently working-class women were unable to access. This means teachers have benefitted from professional privilege (Andrew, 2015) and childcare workers have not, reinforcing the divide between education and care, and between teachers and childcare workers. The replacement of EYPS with EYTS in 2013 should have signalled an end to the divide; however, the opportunity was lost when the government decided that EYTs could not lead maintained nursery or reception classes.

The change from EYPS to EYTS was significant to the participants as it occurred just as they were about to be awarded EYPS. The participants reacted very differently, for example Lauren said, 'EYT it's a good thing, the right to be here, an incentive, it will bring the right people into early years not just primary and secondary'. It is not possible to know if Lauren still thinks this, but she went on to study a Post Graduate Certificate in Education (PGCE) with Qualified Teacher Status (QTS).

Emma had a very different reaction; she stated:

> I'm disappointed, grossly disappointed by the fact that EYPS isn't equivalent to an Early Years Teacher. I would have waited a year to complete EYT instead. Now I don't think I'll bother continuing in higher education, whereas during my EYP I was considering progressing to complete an MA.

Emma felt EYTS had undermined EYPS, although as it turned out EYTs have not gained the professional privilege associated with QTS. This professional privilege has not been achieved because the professional status has not addressed the fundamental schemes of value in relation to gender and class which have positioned childcare workers as less valuable than those who educate. It is not possible for practitioners even with degree level qualifications or above to assume professional status due to their social positioning as part of the childcare workforce. Skeggs (2004) suggests that to change the status and value of childcare workers will require a different strategy of professionalisation from one enjoyed by those with more value. Andrew (2015) draws on this idea to argue that current models of professionalisation are conceptually flawed relying too heavily on qualifications for recognition and should shift to a model which recognises the expertise practitioners' value. However, Nutbrown (2021) argues that qualifications are more than a 'piece of paper or hoop to jump through' (p. 239) to obtain a particular job role in ECEC, at their best they ensure educators have deep knowledge, understanding and skills to provide high-quality ECEC. Nutbrown (2021) also argues that qualifications should stand as evidence of thoughtful, attuned and reflective practice whereby practitioners think about how they interact with children in meaningful 'learning encounters' (p. 240). It is these relational aspects of the work that the participants in Andrew's (2015) research identified as important and the expertise and skill to do this relational work well is described as 'emotional capital' (Andrew, 2015, p. 316), but Andrew reminds us that models relying on relational skills are likely to be devalued, labelled as natural attributes of women.

Conclusion

Professionalisation is ongoing, shaped by local, national and global forces and impeded by the historical and unresolved social positioning of the childcare workforce by virtue of class and gender. The dominant emerging model has been heavily influenced by top-down policy drivers with emphasis on qualifications and accountability measures. Such a technical model of professionalism excludes aspects of practice and expertise which are difficult to measure but are valued by the workforce, including an ethic of care (Osgood, 2006b), relationships and professional love (Page, 2016, 2018). This is not to eschew qualifications; they matter at the level of the individual practitioner, children's outcomes and to quality of practice in the setting. It is possible to conceive a model of professionalism which reflects what is important to practitioners and aligns with models of leadership which are democratic and relational in nature, reliant on influence through collaboration, negotiation and modelling rather than a position of power. Such a professional might be effective in understanding and implementing policy, but it is essential that they are able to critically reflect on, and challenge policy and practice if necessary.

Whilst progress has been made towards professionalisation of the ECEC workforce in the PVI sector in England a significant stumbling block remains, low pay. Pay matters because it sends a visible signal to the workforce and all stakeholders of the value of ECEC. As previously mentioned Bonetti (2019) reported that in real terms wages had gone backwards since 2013 for practitioners in the sector, and the Low Pay Commission (LPC) reported in 2020 that this has been exacerbated by the pandemic, so that one in ten childcare workers are reporting facing considerable hardship with household income below £17,000, and this applied to workers with degrees as well as lower levels of qualification (LPC, 2020). Osgood argued in 2009 that policy discourse on quality in the sector masks the issue of low pay, and this persists. It is ironic that the focus on improving the lives of disadvantaged children and families is at the expense of those working in the sector, so that 10% of the workforce are themselves disadvantaged. The PVI sector is heavily dependent on government funding, so if they are committed to a high-quality service which reduces inequality it should not continue to exploit the workforce. However, other powerful stakeholders such as parents, Ofsted and owners of large, profitable chains of private nurseries could, and should, call for better pay and conditions. It is also necessary for the workforce to come together and articulate their model of professionalism and its real value. This is particularly challenging due to their lack of cultural capital but is possible as illustrated by the workforce in Ireland which is becoming more politicised and have two trade unions campaigning for better pay and conditions (Arndt et al., 2018).

Although it is disappointing that the project to professionalise the ECEC workforce in the PVI sector is far from complete, progress has been made in identifying key factors which are important to practitioners. It is also possible to see how these factors underpin leadership, particularly in relation to improving quality of provision and ultimately outcomes for children. The following chapter explores how externally set expectations and frameworks, including government published and sponsored practice guidance, can be used to develop practice and pedagogic leadership in early years provision, and how this impacts on the autonomy and decisional capital of the early years practitioner.

References

Andrew, Y. (2015). Beyond professionalism: Classed and gendered capital in childcare work. *Contemporary Issues in Early Childhood*, 16 (4), 305–321.

Arndt, S., Urban, M., Murray, C., Smith, K., Swadener, B. and Ellegard, T. (2018). Contesting early childhood identities: A cross-national discussion. *Contemporary Issues in Early Childhood*, 19 (2), 97–116.

Ball, S. (2003). The teacher's soul and the terrors of performativity. *Journal of Education*, 8 (2), 215–228.

Ball, S. (2008). Performativity, privatisation, professionals and the state. In: Cunningham, B. (ed.), *Exploring Professionalism*. London: Bedford Way Papers, 50–72.

Barnett, R. (2008). Critical professionalism in an age of supercomplexity. In: Cunningham, B. (ed.), *Exploring Professionalism*. London: Bedford Way Papers, 190–208.

Bonetti, S. (2019). *The Early Years Workforce in England: A Comparative Analysis Using the Labour Force Survey*. Education Policy Institute and Nuffield Foundation.

Bourdieu, P. (1977). *Outline of a Theory of Practice*. Cambridge: Cambridge University Press.

Bourdieu, P. (1984). *Distinction: A Social Critique of the Judgement of Taste*. London: Sage.

Bourdieu, P. (1992). *The Logic of Practice*. Cambridge: Polity Press.

Campbell-Barr, V. (2018). The silencing of the knowledge-base in early childhood education and care professionalism. *International Journal of Early Years Education*, 26 (1), 75–89. https://doi.org/10.1080/09669760.2017.1414689

Campbell-Barr, V., Georgeson, J., and Selbie, P. (2015). International perspectives on workforce development in ECEC: History, philosophy and politics. In: Campbell-Barr, V., and Georgeson, J. (eds.) *International Perspectives on Work force Development*, pp. 5–11. Northwick: Critical Publishing.

Ceeda (2019). *Independent Research about and for the Early Years Sector*. Last accessed 9/1/21. aboutearlyyears.co.uk

Colmer, K. (2017). Collaborative professional learning: Contributing to the growth of leadership, professional identity and professionalism. *European Early Childhood Education Research Journal*, 25 (3), 436–449.

Crook, D. (2008). Changing modes of teacher professionalism: Traditional, managerial, collaborative and democratic. In: Cunningham, B. (ed.), *Exploring Professionalism*. London: Bedford Way Papers, 50–72.

Department for Education (DfE) (2021). *Statutory Framework for the Early Years Foundation Stage: Setting the standards for learning, development and care for children from birth to five*.

Education Policy Institute (EPI) (2018). Early years education: What does high quality provision look like? Last accessed 3/2/2021 https://epi.org.uk/publications-and-research/early-years-high-quality-provision/

Elfer, P. (2007). Nurseries and emotional well-being: Evaluating an emotionally containing model of professional development. *Early Years*, 27 (3), 267–279.

Elfer, P. (2008). *Children under three and their key adults: relationships to support thinking*. TACTYC Conference Roehampton University.

Elfer, P. (2010). The power of psychoanalytic conceptions in understanding nurseries. *Journal of Infant Observations and It Application*, 13, 59–63.

Hadfield, M. et al. (2012). *First National Survey of Practitioners with EYPS*. Walsall: CeDare and University of Wolverhampton. https://dera.ioe.ac.uk/1847/1/First_National_Survey_of_Practitoners_with_EYPS.pdf

Hordern, J. (2013). A productive system of early years professional development. *Early Years*, 33 (2), 106–118.

Kay, L., Wood, E., Nuttall, J. and Henderson, L. (2021). Problematising policies for workforce reform in early childhood education: A rhetorical analysis of England's Early Years Teacher Status. *Journal of Education Policy*, 36 (2), 179–195. https://doi.org/10.1080/02680939.2019.1637546

Low Pay Commission (LPC) (2020). *National Minimum Wage: Low Pay Commission Report 2020*. London: Crown Publications.

Manning-Morton, J. (2006). The personal is professional: Professionalism and the birth to threes practitioner. *Contemporary Issues in Early Childhood*, 7 (1), 42.

Melhuish, E. and Barnes, J. (2018). Compensatory education. In S. Hupp and J. Jewell (eds.), *The Encyclopedia of Child and Adolescent Development*, 360–370. London: Wiley/Blackwell.

Melhuish, E., Ereky-Stevens, K., Petrogiannis, K., Ariescu, A., Penderi, E., Rentzou, K., Towell, A., Slot, P., Broekhuizen, M. and Leseman, P. (2015). *A Review of Research on the Effect of Early Childhood Education and Care (ECEC) upon Child Development*. CARE Project, Curriculum Quality Analysis and Impact Review of European Early Childhood Education and Care (ECEC).

Melhuish, E. and Gardiner, J. (2018). *Study of Early Education and Development (SEED): Study of Quality in Early Years Provision in England (Revised) Research brief*. London: Department for Education.

Melhuish, E. and Gardiner, J. (2020). *Study of Early Education and Development (SEED): Impact Study on Early Education Use and Child Outcomes Up to Age Five Years. Research brief*. London: Department for education.

Noddings, N. (1984). *Caring: A Feminine Approach to Ethics and Moral Education*. Berkeley, CA: University of California Press.

Nutbrown, C. (2021). Early childhood educators' qualifications: A framework for change. *International Journal of Early Years Education*, 29 (3), 236–249. https://doi.org/10.1080/09669760.2021.1892601

Oberheumer, P. (2005). Conceptualising the early childhood pedagogue: Policy approaches and issues of professionalism. *European Early Childhood Education Research Journal*, 13 (1), 5–16.

Ofsted (2021). Early Years Inspection Handbook for Ofsted-registered Provision. Ofsted Early years inspection handbook for Ofsted-registered provision - GOV.UK (www.gov.uk)

Osgood, J. (2006a). Professionalism and performativity: The feminist challenge facing early years practitioners. *Early Years*, 26(2), 187–199.

Osgood, J. (2006b). Rethinking professionalism in the early years: Perspectives from the United Kingdom. *Contemporary Issues in Early Childhood*, 7 (1), 1–4.

Osgood, J. (2009). Childcare workforce reform in England and the' early years professional': A critical discourse analysis. *Journal of Education Policy*, 24 (6), 733–751.

Osgood, J. (2010). Reconstructing professionalism in ECEC: The case for the 'critically reflective emotional professional'. *Early Years: An International Research Journal*, 30 (2), 119–133.

Page, J. (2016). Educators perspectives on attachment and professional love in early years settings in England. In White, E. J., and Dalli, C. (eds.) *Under-Three Year Olds in Policy and Practice*. Gateway East, Singapore: Springer, pp. 131–142.

Page, J. (2017). Reframing infant-toddler pedagogy through a lens of professional love: Exploring narratives of professional practice in early childhood settings in England. *Contemporary Issues in Early Childhood*, 18 (4), 387–399.

Page, J. (2018). Characterising the principles of Professional Love in early childhood care and education. *International Journal of Early Years Education*, 26 (2), 125–141.

Payler, J. and Locke, R. (2013). Disrupting communities of practice? How 'reluctant' practitioners view early years workforce reform in England. *European Early Childhood Education Research Journal*, 21 (1), 125–138.

Ritzer, G. (2001). *Explorations in Social Theory*. London: Sage.

Rodd, J. (1998). *Leadership in Early Childhood*. Maidenhead: Open University Press.

Rodd, J. (2013). *Leadership in Early Childhood: The Pathway to Professionalism* (3rd ed.). Maidenhead: Open University Press.

Schon, D. (1992). The crisis of professional knowledge and the pursuit of an epistemology of practice. *Journal of Interprofessional Care*, 6 (1), 49–63.

Sims, M., Forrest, R., Semann, A. and Slattery, C. (2015). Conceptions of early childhood leadership: Driving new professionalism. *International Journal of Leadership in Education: Theory and Practice*, 18 (2), 149–166.

Skeggs, B. (1997). *Formations of Class and Gender*. London: Sage.

Skeggs, B. (2004). *Class, Self, Culture*. London: Routledge.

Stephens, P. (2009). The nature of social pedagogy: An excursion in Norwegian territory. *Child and Family Social Work*, 14, 343–351.

Sylva, K., Melhuish, E., Sammons, P., Siraj-Blatchford, I. and Taggart, B. (2010). *Early Childhood Matters: Evidence from the Effective Pre-School and Primary Education Project*. Oxon: Routledge.

Taggart, G. (2011). Don't we care? The ethics and emotional labour of early years professionalism. *Early Years*, 31 (1), 85–95.

Vrinioti, K. (2013). Professionalisation in early childhood education: A comparative view of emerging. *European Early Childhood Education Research Journal*, 21 (1), 150–163.

Whitty, G. (2008). Changing modes of teacher professionalism: Traditional, managerial, collaborative and democratic. In: Cunningham, B. (ed.), *Exploring Professionalism*. London: Bedford Way Papers, 144–160.

Chapter 6

Practice standards and the shaping of professional identity

Technicians or creative researchers?

Introduction

This chapter considers the role of the practitioner in response to changing discourse concerning the purpose of early years provision. It examines the ECEC professional standards and competencies that graduate professionals are expected to meet, and considers how these align with the conceptualisations of professionalism discussed in Chapter 5, and discusses whether they reflect what is identified as important by graduate professionals. In particular, this chapter concludes by considering how practice guidance and frameworks not only focus on statutory minimal standards for practice, but also may limit the voice and decisional capital of the practitioner and how this is perpetuated by the current terms and conditions of service for practitioners, and entry requirements for their employment and professional education.

Policy changes and early years discourse

Changes to the discourse of early years practice emerged from the Every Child Matters (ECM) outcomes (DfES, 2004), new requirements for multi-agency working (Laming, 2003; DfES, 2004) and the introduction of the EYFS (DCSF, 2008). The demands of the ECM outcomes initially placed care and the promotion of social and emotional well-being on an equal footing with positive educational outcomes, and increased emphasis on family support, required strong interpersonal and communication skills. The changing policy agenda for early years provision also meant that practitioners needed a more detailed and critical understanding of health, education and safeguarding policy and their interpretation. The more recent focus on school readiness, evidenced through children's achievement of Early Learning Goals, particularly for literacy and maths, now places more emphasis on the role of practitioner as educator, accountable for ensuring all children achieve a 'good level of development' as they move into Key Stage 1. Over the last 20 years this had led to changes not only to required levels of qualification, but also to considerable debate about what knowledge base practitioners require and what practice skills, leading to different constructions of their professional identity and status.

Following the publication of the government's childcare strategy (DfES, 1998), it became clear that a more qualified workforce was required, and the ECM agenda of 2004 also identified the need for additional skills enabling practitioners to contribute effectively to multi-agency working and family support roles. Existing levels of qualification across the sector were low, and training opportunities for unqualified staff were either limited or costly. Professional development provision either took the form

DOI: 10.4324/9780367815387-6

of competence-based, workplace training that allowed practitioners to evidence their skill and knowledge through their practice, or else it was college-based with a substantial placement element to enable students to apply their knowledge of theory to practice. This training only offered qualification to Level 3 at most, where the emphasis lay on ensuring practitioners understood their role in relation to regulatory frameworks and practice remained subject to oversight from inspectors, advisory teachers and local authority development teams. The new discourses of practice suggested that change managers and leaders of pedagogy were required to ensure the government's agenda, for early intervention to address children's needs and well-being and a pro-active approach to tackling educational disadvantage and ensuring school readiness, could be met.

Workforce reform initiatives

Workforce reform policy at that time (DfES, 2006), as has already been stated, characterised the current workforce as lacking expert knowledge and skill, and funding was introduced to enable practitioners to address this, but only to Level 3. The workforce development strategy that followed the new Childcare Strategy (DfEE, 1998) provided funding for unqualified practitioners to achieve the now mandated Level 3 qualifications, with an emphasis on competence-based qualifications, supported and assessed in the workplace, with varying levels of access to underpinning knowledge teaching. Practitioners were able to demonstrate their understanding of children's developmental and learning needs through observed practice, and their awareness and understanding of theory, policy and legislation through questioning and discussion. Their mentors and assessors were mostly their more senior, Level 3 qualified colleagues within the same organisation, whose judgements were overseen and verified by representatives from local colleges and/or training agencies. Judgements about appropriate and competent practice required the candidate to justify their actions in the context of theory, policy and legislation. Deeper critical reflection, on the appropriateness of these frameworks rather than the operationalisation of them, does not form part of the Level 3 qualification or knowledge base, encouraging a professional identity based on compliance and implementation rather than critical understanding and interpretation.

To address the need for change managers and pedagogical leadership to raise the quality of provision, foundation degrees (offering qualification at Level 5), with top-ups and accreditation routes to BA Hons (Level 6) and EYPS, were then introduced with an emphasis on critical reflection (DfES, 2006; CWDC, 2008). Sector endorsement of these higher-level qualifications ensured a common core to their content that included critical reflection and self-evaluation, and a meaningful link to current early years practice, as well as supporting the development of leadership skills for their students. Collaboration between the early years sector and government through the Teachers Agency, and later the NCTL, supported their credibility in preparing effective leaders who would raise quality to meet the expectations of regulators. But what was missing was a national infrastructure for the sector, which would support career development and progression, through shared and nationally recognised job descriptions, senior posts including the Foundation degree qualified Senior Practitioner originally envisioned by the government and appropriate terms and conditions of employment to underpin these. In particular, parity with schoolteachers, for delivering what was increasingly been presented as an education service subject to government oversight and regulation, was, and still is, missing for early years practitioners with degrees, EYPS and EYTS accreditation, and considerable years of experience.

The continued lack of follow-through from the original workforce reform proposals to introduce nationally the role of the Senior Practitioner, qualified to Level 5, and the lack of a mandate for graduate led provision across the sector, both indicate that higher-level, critically reflective qualifications remain at best desirable, and might even potentially be viewed as an expensive luxury. At the same time, the retaining of Level 3 as the only mandated standard for practice, and only for a limited number of staff within a setting (DfE, 2021), along with a static level of funding for nursery education provision, reinforces the perception that a minimal standard of qualification is acceptable. The most recent workforce strategy document (DfE, 2017) has done nothing to raise aspirations regarding graduate leadership of practice, continuing to emphasise the importance of ensuring minimum levels of qualification are met. Level 2 qualifications have been described by Nutbrown (2012) as an appropriate entry to early years practice, and acknowledged as valuable in offering a gateway to Level 3 qualification, but considered as insufficient to guarantee good practice in settings, yet current registration requirements allow for half the staff in a setting to hold either Level 2 or no qualification at all. The importance of a good knowledge of Maths and English is acknowledged for practitioners to support literacy and maths in the EYFS. However, the acceptable level of qualification for EYEs is the bare minimum of Level 2 functional skills qualifications, which include 'the most necessary' skills and knowledge, rather than the breadth that would be included in the GCSE passes required for Qualified Teacher Status. The argument advanced for this, that if GCSEs were required this might significantly reduce the applicant pool for early years employment and apprenticeships, implies that willing hands are more valued than knowledgeable practitioners.

This argument, along with the lack of a mandate for graduate-led provision, serves to reinforce the perception of the early years practitioner as a practical and compliant technician rather than a critically reflective expert who is prepared to engage with theory and research to meet young children's needs. The overarching concern for capacity within the workforce seems to privilege sufficiency of places for working parents over the quality of provision or the experience of the child. The lack of career progression for the workforce suggests that their service is perceived to have limited value, and can be appropriately quality assured through compliance with regulatory frameworks so that further study or expertise is superfluous to requirements. Whilst it might be unreasonable to require that all practitioners are graduates, an inconsistent and fluctuating approach to the necessity of graduate leadership for practice has presented the workforce, their employers and their service users with a confused message about the knowledge and skill required for early years work, and the professionalism and agency of practitioners in determining good practice.

The Nutbrown review

In 2012, this confusion, further fuelled by the number and range of qualifications held across the workforce, led the government to commission a review of early years training. Cathy Nutbrown's review (Nutbrown, 2012) identified a number of issues regarding workforce qualifications, including particular concerns over the rigour and depth of some qualification, a decline in standards, insufficient content, particularly in relation to SEND, inclusion and diversity, and a mistrust of some qualifications by employers and parents. She further identified the need for more teaching on critical reflection and pedagogical leadership, to raise expectations of this workforce regarding their knowledge and understanding of holistic development and play, and their ability to respond sensitively to the individual needs of young children. She concluded in her review that Level 3 was the only appropriate qualification to enable practitioners to work without supervision, and that Level 2 qualifications were insufficient other than an introductory gateway to Level 3 training.

Level 3 qualifications and professionalisation

When Cathy Nutbrown was tasked by the government to review qualifications in early education and childcare in 2012, she found that there were 'literally hundreds' (Nutbrown, 2012, p. 6) of qualifications, and she expressed grave doubts that they all covered the knowledge and skills required in practice. Some of these qualifications were distrusted by the sector, and often unfavourably compared with the Certificate or Diploma in Childcare Practice issued by the National Nursery Examination Board (NNEB) between 1945 and 1990. This qualification was considered by the sector to be the 'gold standard' of training for practitioners, comprising academic and practical knowledge of child development, play and health and care routines. In her narrative, one early years practitioner, Karen summarises the high regard for the NNEB qualification and the subsequent distrust of the many newer qualifications saying,

> There weren't the same opportunities then to go to university but getting the NNEB was something to be proud of. That's what Mrs McMahon the tutor used to say, 'Be proud of your qualification.' And it was hard to get in; you went to college, there were only 40 places. All through school, my options were geared towards getting a place; I did childcare, human biology and history. It's not like that now; anyone can get a level 3.

Nutbrown (2012) focused primarily on Level 3 qualifications, and the report is significant because it sets out in detail the skills and knowledge required at Level 3. As such, it acts as a starting point for graduate professional knowledge and skills, enabling all stakeholders, including graduate professionals, to reflect on what distinguishes a Level 3 practitioner from a Level 6 graduate professional. This chapter returns to this discussion on page 81.

Nutbrown (2012) proposed the following as the fundamental structure for Level 3 qualifications (p. 23):

Curriculum:

- a thorough understanding of child development that makes up at least 60% of any course and including:
  - child development and learning from birth to seven – including issues of attachment, social development, health and well-being, neuroscience, and brain development
  - learning theories, and cognitive development
  - Special educational needs and disability issues
  - Language development and play

- an understanding and explanation of responsibilities in relation to
  - safeguarding and child protection issues
  - health and safety
  - nutrition,
  - basic first aid
  - legal obligations and duties
- issues of diversity and inclusion, including how every child can be given the best possible early years experience, paying due attention to their background and heritage, and welcoming and supporting different types of families
- an understanding of the importance of working in partnership with parents to support their children's learning and development
- the application of knowledge in a reflective and appropriate way, differentiating between the needs of each child.

Pedagogical processes:

- Equip students with the skills to undertake and reflect on observations and assessments, and to know how to use these effectively and appropriately, and to share them with parents.
- Ensure that students undertake good quality learning placements, in at least three different and appropriate settings, to last a total equivalent of a minimum of 20% of the total course duration.
- Equip students with an understanding of why engaging families in a two-way process is important and equip students with the skills to do this effectively.

Other:

- Demonstrate that it has valid, reliable assessment and awarding procedures (via external scrutiny).
- Demand that students enrolling on courses have an acceptable level of English and mathematics.

This structure would introduce the practitioner to the specialist knowledge that underpins practice and provision for children from birth to seven years old. However, the emphasis remains on what to do and how to do it, the acquisition of specific skills and the application of knowledge to practice. This reflects a commonly held assumption in work-based learning, that the elements of successful practice in a given occupation can be specified in advance, and delivered in formal training (Hager, 2011), often resulting in a competence-based approach to training that relies on a close alignment between professional practice standards, the curriculum of the training course and the use of practicums or work-experience placements. Such an approach encourages a perception of practice skills as generic and applicable to any given situation, on the assumption that all workplaces are similar, and that all practice situations are predictable, assumptions that Nutbrown (2012), amongst others, has been keen to challenge.

This structure, along with a competence based approach supported by underpinning knowledge, and the level of the qualification itself (NVQ 3 equates A level, and is well below the graduate-level qualification required for those working in compulsory education), continues to locate good practice as emerging from beyond the sector, through the received wisdom of published research and theory, particularly from sources approved by awarding bodies and practice regulators. By limiting the scope of reflection to a judgement of successful differentiation of practice to meet children's individual needs, it limited opportunity for practitioners to see themselves as contributors to their practice knowledge base, positioning them as implementers of theory rather than interpreters. It also introduced the practitioner to the fundamental communication and interpersonal skills, but presented these as essential tools for effective partnership and multi-agency working rather than as being fundamental elements of a relational approach to professionalism and professional identity. Finally, this proposed structure emphasises the need for external credibility in how such a qualification is awarded, introducing quality assurance mechanisms led by education-based authorities outside the early years sector, rather than calling on the sector itself to judge the rigour and validity of training provision.

This proposal for this fundamental content of the Level 3 course was made some six years post the introduction of EYPS and more than ten years after the introduction of Foundation degrees in Early Years. Nutbrown (2012) acknowledged that the Foundation degree, with its sector endorsement, was a robust qualification and that EYPs were making a positive contribution to improving children's outcomes (a finding also identified by Mathers et al. 2011). This review of Level 3 qualification content, it could be argued, represented an attempt to ensure that these not only offered practitioners the knowledge and skill they needed to begin their careers but also furnished them with a secure base and the initial skills to progress to more critically oriented professional education, and further career development. However, it could further be argued that Nutbrown's review was too late as the entrenched distrust of the quality of Level 3 qualifications, and the lack of a clearly articulated career progression route from practitioner to professional, had undermined the professionalisation project. Nevertheless, Nutbrown (2012) articulated several other issues which continue to undermine professionalisation in ECEC, including low levels of literacy and numeracy in the workforce, recruitment practices onto courses described as the 'hair or care stereotype' (2012, p. 9) whereby girls with the lowest academic qualifications are steered towards childcare or hairdressing, and the lack of parity between EYPS and QTS.

The government did, in part, accept and act on Nutbrown's recommendations, by replacing EYPS with EYTS and introducing Early Years Educators (EYEs) at Level 3 (DfE, 2013). This was an attempt to raise the quality of Level 3 qualifications by insisting that all EYEs should have a grade C or equivalent in GCSE in English and Maths. It is unfortunate that attempts to align early years practitioner qualifications with the requirements for teachers have been successfully challenged on the basis that these threaten recruitment to the sector, rather than on the basis that such roles do not offer parity in terms of conditions of service. The apparent threat posed by the requirement to have a Maths GCSE at grade C or equivalent was sufficient to ensure it was quickly dropped. However, the lack of parity for EYTS with QTS with respect to its acceptability in schools to run Reception classes, and with pay, working conditions and status continues is still discussed, although with little sign of the status quo being altered. That there are fewer and fewer graduates entering or remaining in the early years workforce is clearly less of a concern while ever there is no mandate for graduate-led provision.

EYPS

Although EYPS has been replaced by EYTS, it is useful to examine aspects of the EYPS standards to draw out the key differences between the Level 3 practitioner and the Level 6 professional and to discuss how the professional was framed by the standards. The Level 3 practitioner is required to have a sound understanding of holistic development and the legal framework for practice, so that children's learning and development are supported, and their safety and well-being protected. The focus of their role is practice within the setting, team leadership as their experience grows, and compliance with organisational policy and national legislation. The graduate practitioner (at this point an EYP) was expected to develop this focus through their critical reflection on theory and policy and how these apply to practice, managing change to improve children's experience of provision and their overall educational outcomes.

There were originally 39 standards organised into 6 areas: knowledge and understanding; effective practice; relationships with children; communicating and working in partnership with families and carers; teamwork and collaboration; and professional development (Roberts-Holmes, 2013). There were many overlaps between the 39 standards for EYPS and Nutbrown's fundamental content at Level 3, including a thorough knowledge of child development and of the principles and content of EYFS; working in partnership with parents and the use of observation to monitor children's progress and inform planning. It could be argued that although the EYP was understood to be a leader and change manager, they were also a practitioner who spent much of their working day with the children, and remained close to the practice they were there to reflect on and improve. The EYP standards reflected the centrality of their relationship with children and their families to their role. However, EYPS was symbolic of the attempt to provide integrated ECEC along with multi-agency professional working (Roberts-Holmes, 2013), and so unlike the Level 3 practitioner EYPs were expected to look beyond the setting and play a key role in multi-agency professional working as set out in standard 36:

> To contribute to the work of a multi-professional team and where appropriate coordinate and implement agreed programmes and interventions on a day-to-day basis.
>
> (CWDC, 2008, p. 95)

A further key difference was that the EYP was expected to be accountable for the delivery of high-quality provision (Standard 24) and to help colleagues develop and improve their practice. This was encapsulated in the overarching vision for the role of the EYP as an 'agent of change', whereby all the standards carried expectations of transformational leadership activity to change practice and raise standards of professionalism (Murray and McDowell Clark, 2013).

Although there was a greater expectation for critical reflection on the context and content of practice, however, setting standards for the role of the EYP (with further subdivisions to clarify the detail about how these could be met) presents it as a series of competences to meet. Again, this implies a role with a set of generic skills and behaviours that can be applied to any specific context, so that successful accreditation as a professional is based on the justification of practice determined through externally set standards rather than personally held professional values. Osgood (2010) argued that this rational external model of the EYP embodied in the standards exerted a dominating influence on the emerging professional, what Evetts (2011) describes as a 'from above' approach to professionalisation. Whilst this appears to foster autonomy and agency in judgements about practice, Evetts argues that it actually constrains the practitioner by requiring them to demonstrate their own compliance with externally set standards and requirements. Murray (2013) found this to be at odds with their internal beliefs and perceptions of professionalism, which held 'passionate care' (p. 538) at its core. It is interesting, then, that when compared with the later EYTS standards (NCTL, 2013), the last iteration of the EYPS standards (TA, 2012) seems in comparison to present a construction of professionalism that is much more focused on the needs of the child and the quality of the practitioner–child relationship than the standards designed by the NCTL. Unfortunately, the workforce did not have time to work out the tension between the external and internal models of professionalism to develop and articulate their own model, that could have encapsulated their core beliefs and brought external social legitimacy (Murray, 2013), as EYPS was replaced by EYTS within six years.

EYTS

Early Years Teacher Status represents the DfE construction of the role of the lead practitioner in early years practice, reflecting how early years provision was now positioned as a vehicle primarily to ensure school readiness through the achievement of Early Learning Goals. Rather than considering the holistic development of young children as the core of early years practice, Kay et al. (2021) point to an ideological shift, first identified in More Great Childcare (DfE, 2013), from a focus on the quality of the child's experience of ECEC to a more marketed and commoditised version of ECEC, with the emphasis on educational outcomes. Attention was now focused on the role of the practitioner in preparing children for formal compulsory education, the early identification of additional learning needs and the compilation of national data sets for measuring children's early learning progress. Furthermore, closer analysis of the wording, content and organisation of the original EYTS standards (NCTL, 2013) indicates a particular construction of the lead practitioner in early years provision today that is quite different from the construction offered by the previous EYPS standards of 2012.

The first column of Table 6.1 lists Early Years Professional Status Standards in order taken from Teachers Agency (2012); the second column lists the Early Years Teacher Standards in order taken from NCTL (2013).

The EYTS standards place greater and more immediate emphasis on the effective delivery of the EYFS curriculum framework, evidenced through assessment of the children against early learning goals, rather than the development of positive relationships with children and the effective partnership working with parents and carers. Meeting policy and legal requirements would appear to be foregrounded over a focus on children's social and emotional needs and family support, reflecting the change in discourse regarding the practitioner role since 2013 when Teacher and Educator job titles were introduced by government (DfE, 2013). The role of the practitioner as a leader of practice and change could also be argued to be diluted as the wording of the current standards seems to focus on personal compliance with required standards, and the modelling

Table 6.1 EYPS and EYTS standards

EYPS Standards (Teachers Agency, 2012)	EYTS Standards (NCTL, 2013)
1 Support the healthy growth and development of children from birth to the age of five.	1 Set high expectations which inspire, motivate and challenge all children.
2 Work directly with children and in partnership with their families to facilitate learning and support development.	2 Promote good progress and outcomes by children.
3 Safeguard and promote the welfare of children.	3 Demonstrate good knowledge of early learning and EYFS.
4 Set high expectations which inspire, motivate and challenge every child.	4 Plan education and care taking account of the needs of all children.
5 Make use of observation and assessment to meet the individual needs of every child.	5 Adapt education and care to respond to the strengths and needs of all children.
6 Plan provision taking account of the individual needs of every child	6 Make accurate and productive use of assessment.
7 Fulfil wider professional responsibilities by promoting positive partnership working to support the child.	7 Safeguard and promote the welfare of children, and provide a safe learning environment.
8 Lead practice and foster a culture of continuous improvement.	8 Fulfil wider professional responsibilities.

of one's own practice, rather than the leading of a team to determine and embed good practice. The previous EYPS standards reflected a perception of the lead practitioner as accountable first and foremost for the professional judgements they make about the child and their individual learning and development needs, for their work in supporting families, and then for their team working and collegiality both within and beyond the setting, within the policy and legal context for provision.

However, the originally envisaged Early Years Professional, critically reflective, self-aware and capable of managing change, it could be argued, no longer fits the current perception of the practitioner role in preparing children for Key Stage 1 and formal learning. Instead, the practitioner now must pay close attention to the demands of Key Stage 1 curriculum and pedagogy and fit their practice to prepare children appropriately. The current assessment agenda for early years, and revised practice guidance and curriculum framework now position early years provision as subordinate to compulsory schooling rather than as a benefit to children's holistic development, and construct the role and identity of the practitioner accordingly. Overall, these frameworks and the current EYTS standards construct a lead practitioner as accountable for their compliance with curriculum documents and the legal framework for practice.

Graduate Practitioner Competencies

In a bid to wrestle the ECEC graduate professional back from a compliance oriented, teacher modelled profession, the Early Childhood Studies Degree Network (ECSDN) introduced the Graduate Practitioner Competencies (ECGPC) in 2019 which were subsequently revised in 2020. The ECSDN is a network of institutions which offer Early Childhood Studies degrees, and one of their aims is to campaign for a high-status early childhood graduate profession. The competencies are practice-based and assessed at Level 6, and it is hoped that they will provide a consistent benchmark for the sector, removing confusion about how the degree programmes align with practice. As the competencies are new and because many students were unable to access placements during the pandemic it is too early to report on their effect in the sector; however, it is important to include them here as they signal some resistance to the dominant teacher modelled professional. These competencies are set out in Table 6.2 alongside the EYT standards.

The first column lists Early childhood Graduate Practitioner Competencies in order taken from ECSDN (2020); the second column lists the Early Years Teacher Standards in order taken from NCTL (2013).

The Early Childhood Graduate Practitioner (ECGP) is conceived first and foremost as an advocate for the child's rights and participation, and the child is framed as an active co-constructor of their own learning, whereas the EYT is expected to be concerned with the child's education above all else and the child is framed as the passive recipient of adult planned learning opportunities. The ECGPCs are rooted in a democratic social justice framework whilst the EYT as an individual is required to be honest and act with integrity. Furthermore, the EYT is expected to be leading education and care, but there is much less emphasis on leadership for the ECGP and a greater expectation to work collaboratively. Conceptually the ECGP is close to the critically reflective, democratic professional or the early childhood pedagogue described by Oberhuemer (2005) which emphasises the social and cultural aspects of the role and not just the educational dimension. However, as far back as 2005 the role of the early

Table 6.2 ECGPC statements and EYT standards

ECGPC (ECSDN, 2020)	EYT Standards (NCTL, 2013)
Advocating for young children's rights and participation.	Set high expectations which inspire, motivate and challenge all children.
Promote holistic child development.	Promote good progress and outcomes by children.
Work directly with young children, families and colleagues to promote health, well-being, safety and nurturing care.	Demonstrate good knowledge of early learning and EYFS.
Observe, listen and plan for young children to support their well-being, early learning, progression and transitions.	Plan education and care taking account of the needs of all children.
Safeguarding and child protection.	Adapt education and care to respond to the strengths and needs of all children.
Inclusive practice.	Make accurate and productive use of assessment.
Partnership with parents and caregivers.	Safeguard and promote the welfare of children and provide a safe learning environment.
Collaborating with others.	Fulfil wider professional responsibilities.
Professional development.	

childhood pedagogue was threatened by the introduction of an early childhood curriculum and tighter accountability measures in Germany, Sweden and Norway. In Sweden practitioners became known as early childhood teachers (Oberhuemer, 2005), so it is very difficult to see how the ECGPCs will be able to counter the dominant discourse that professionalism in early years practice is best served by adult-directed learning.

By centring workforce reform and professional development on qualifications structured as sets of competences to be achieved, and where underpinning knowledge was assumed to be demonstrated through practice rather than by critical discussion, early years practice is then presented as a technical rational series of skills, to be learnt free of context and then applied consistently across a range of situations. This overlooks the fundamental point made very clearly by Nutbrown (2012) in her proposed structure for Level 3 qualifications, that early years practice is a complex endeavour, requiring an understanding of and a sensitivity to children's individual developmental needs, rather than a series of steps that can be applied to any child in any context. Whilst the assessment regime for both the college-based provision and work-based learning qualifications allows space for innovation and initiative to be applied to practice, a candidate's success in their training relied on approval from a current practitioner, within a specific professional context, often with the power of a managerial role, encouraging a culture of compliance to maintain a place within or ensure acceptance into an existing community of practice.

Moss (2006) had earlier denounced such an approach as overlooking the complexity of supporting and promoting young children's learning and development, and ignoring the vital contribution of experience, professional judgement and critical reflection on theory to effective practice, an argument he returned to in his critique of international comparison studies (Moss et al., 2016). He argues instead for practitioners to be understood as creative researchers, applying specialist knowledge to their interactions with individual children, families and colleagues on the basis of critical reflection, and using the ensuing experience to build a practice-driven knowledge base. This much more agentic and autonomous construction of the role of the practitioner establishes early years practice as a field in its own right rather than as a servant of formal education, and the practitioner as a knowledgeable specialist, capable of contributing to a dynamic and child-centred rather than curriculum-driven knowledge base.

Conclusion

It is not only the content, pedagogy and level of the initial vocation education of practitioners that serve to perpetuate their restricted capital and autonomy as professionals, but also context of their practice and employment. Agentic professionals also need the freedom to make autonomous decisions with regard to practice and to interpret regulatory frameworks and shape practice to meet the needs of children as individuals – what Hargreaves and Fullan (2012) have described as decisional capital. Whilst Foundation and full BA Hons ECS degrees can (and do) teach the value and processes of reflection on practice, and the critical analysis of theory and research, the early years setting must still comply with government's regulatory frameworks, and demonstrate its effectiveness in meeting targets and outcomes to maintain funding. Guidance documents endorsed by the DfE for good practice are still set out in a format that suggests a universal developmental pathway for all children, with little reference to underpinning theory to support practitioners in making their own judgements about children's individual developmental trajectories and the need for further intervention. The framing of such guidance as a pathway to a universal learning goal, with identified 'points for observation' (DfE, 2021) along the way, reduces the scope for practitioners to exercise their own judgement about the need for assessment, and undermines their confidence in making their own interpretation of research, theory, and the behaviour of the child in front of them. The current national assessment agenda for children in the early years, along with growing concern about children's capacity to meet learning targets after two years of interrupted and socially distanced learning, focuses on the importance of literacy and mathematical understanding, and readiness for formal schooling, undermining practitioners' understanding of what young children need for healthy holistic development and how best it might be achieved. This curriculum outcome-driven approach can have the effect of focussing critical reflection at a more superficial level (Goodman, 1984) of evaluating the outcomes of practice, rather than its underpinning values and principles (Moss, 2012; Roberts-Holmes & Bradbury, 2016), limiting the voice of the practitioner to the articulation of orthodox received knowledge (Johns, 2004), rather than encouraging them to contribute to the development of new knowledge within their field.

Hargreaves and Fullan (2012) argue that the professionalisation of an education workforce requires not only the development of human capital, achieved by offering professional training and education to individual members of a workforce, but also an increase in social and decisional capital. However, the government's approach to up-skilling its apparently deficient workforce was centred on just such an increase of individuals' knowledge, without significant change to the infrastructure and career pathways within the sector, or the regulatory context for practice. This lack of sector infrastructure in particular would appear now to be a significant threat to the identity and professionalism of the early years practitioner. The standards required to meet EYTS are almost identical to those required for QTS (Kay et al., 2021) with EYTs being identified as graduate leaders responsible for organising and leading high-quality teaching practice and expected to critically reflect as pedagogical leaders on all aspects of early years provision (Boardman, 2020). However, Kay et al. (2021) argue that whilst there is a clear alignment between the EYTS and QTS, it is without the equivalent financial rewards, career progression and professional status. This has profound consequences for professionalisation in the sector as articulated by Bonetti (2018, p. 4) who speculated that 'the early years workforce in the future could be even less qualified than today'. This prediction now appears to be borne out by the figures collected by Archer and Merrick (2020), who reported that the number of Level 3 qualified staff has fallen from 66% in 2017–2018 to 52% in 2018–2019, the number of EYTS from 13 to 5% and the number of unqualified staff has risen from 10 to 26%. This is accompanied by falling levels of recruitment in registrations on EYT courses from 2300 in 2013–14 to under 400 in 2019–2020 (Archer and Merrick, 2020).

Altogether, this indicates a reduction in the number of qualified staff in the workforce, enabled and supported by an adherence to minimal standards for qualifications and professional education, and a strong regulatory context for practice. Whilst Chapter 3 considered the significance of this for professional identity and the social capital and habitus of the practitioner, the next chapter goes on to explore how this worrying trend in workforce qualifications and expertise might be addressed.

References

Archer, N. and Merrick, B. (2020). *Getting the Balance Right: Quality and Quantity in Early Education and Childcare*. The Sutton Trust.

Boardman, K. (2020). Early Years teachers as leaders of change through reflexivity praxis? *Early Child Development and Care*, 190 (3), 322–332.

Bonetti, S. (2018). *The Early Years Workforce: A Fragmented Picture*. Education Policy Institute. [online] Last accessed 25/7/22. https://epi.org.uk/publications-and-research/early-years-workforce_analysis/

Children's Workforce Development Counci (CWDC) (2008). *Guidance to the Standards for the Award of EYPS*. London: CWDC.

Department for Children, Schools and Families (DCSF) (2008). *The Statutory Framework for the Early Years Foundation Stage*. Nottingham: DCSF.

Department for Education and Employment (DfEE) (1998). *The National Childcare Strategy: Meeting the Childcare Challenge*. London: HMSO.

Department for Education and Skills (DfES) (2006). *Children's Workforce Strategy: A Strategy to Build a World Class Workforce for Children And Young People-consultation document*. Nottingham, DfES. [online] Last accessed 25/7/22. https://core.ac.uk/download/pdf/4156097.pdf

DfE (2013). *More Great Childcare: Raising Quality and Giving Parents More Choice*. Crown Copyright.

DfE (2017). *Statutory Framework for the Early Years Foundation Stage: Setting the Standards for Learning, Development and Care for Children from Birth to Five*. London: Crown Copyright.

DfE (2021). *Statutory Framework for the Early Years Foundation Stage*. Crown copyright: 2021.

DfES (2004). *Every Child Matters: Change for Children*. Nottingham: DfES Publications.

Early Childhood Studies Degree Network (ECSDN) (2020). Early Childhood Graduate Degree Competencies. [Online] Last accessed 16/12/21. https://www.ecsdn.org/competencies/

Evetts, J. (2011). A new professionalism? Challenges and opportunities. *Current Sociology*, 59 (4), 406–422.

Goodman, J. (1984). Reflection and teacher education: A case study and theoretical analysis. *Interchanges*, 15, 9–26.

Hager, P. (2011). Refurbishing MacIntyre's account of practice. *Journal of Philosophy of Education*, 45, 545–562.

Johns, C. (2004). *Becoming a Reflective Practitioner* (2nd ed.). Oxford: Blackwell Publishing.

Kay, L., Wood, E., Nuttall, J. and Henderson, L. (2021). Problematising policies for workforce reform in early childhood education: A rhetorical analysis of England's Early Years Teacher Status. *Journal of Education Policy*, 36 (2), 179–195. https://doi.org/10.1080/02680939.2019.1637546

Laming, Lord H. (2003). *The Victoria Climbie Inquiry: Report on an inquiry by Lord Laming*. London: HMSO.

Mathers, S., Ranns, H., Karemaker, A., Moody, A., Sylva K., Graham, J., and Siraj-Blatchford, I. (2011). *Evaluation of the Graduate Leader Fund Final Report*. DfE [online] last accessed 10/3/22. https://www.gov.uk/government/publications/evaluation-of-the-graduate-leader-fund-final-report

Moss, P. (2006). Structure, understandings and discourses: Possibilities for re-envisioning the early childhood worker. *Contemporary Issues in Early Childhood*, 7 (1), 30–41.

Moss, P. (2012). Readiness, partnership, a meeting place? Some thoughts on the possible relationships between early childhood and compulsory school education. *Forum*, 54 (3), 355–368.

Moss, P., Dahlberg, G., Grieshaber, S. et al. (2016). The organisation for economic co-operation and development's international early learning study: Opening for debate and contestation. *Contemporary Issues in Early Childhood*, 17 (3): 343–351.

Murray, J. (2013). Becoming an early years professional: Developing a new professional identity. *European Early Childhood Education Research Journal*, 21 (4), 527–540.

Murray, J. and McDowall Clark, R. (2013). Reframing Leadership as a Participative Pedagogy: The working theories of early years professionals. *Early Years*, 33 (3), 289–301.

National College for Teaching and Leadership (NCTL) (2013). *Teachers' Standards (Early Years)*. [online] Last accessed 25/7/22 NCTL external template (publishing.service.gov.uk)

Nutbrown, C. (2012). *Foundations for Quality: The Independent Review of Early Education and Childcare Qualifications Final Report*. London: Crown Copyright.

Oberhuemer, P. (2005). Conceptualising the Early Childhood Pedagogue: Policy Approaches and Issues of Professionalism. *European Early Childhood and Education Research Journal*, 13 (1), 5–16.

Osgood, J. (2010). Reconstructing professionalism in ECEC: the case for the 'critically reflective emotional professional'. *Early Years: An International Research Journal*, 30 (2), 119–133.

Roberts-Holmes, G. (2013). The English Early Years Professional Status (EYPS) and the split Early Childhood Education and Care (ECEC) system. *European Early Childhood Education Research Journal*, 21 (3), 339–353.

Roberts-Holmes, G. and Bradbury, A. (2016). The datafication of early years education and its impact upon pedagogy. *Improving Schools*, 19 (2), 119–128. https://doi.org/10.1177/1365480216651519

Teachers Agency (TA) (2012). *Teachers' Standards (early years)*. [online] Last accessed 25/7/22. https://www.gov.uk/government/publications/early-years-teachers-standards

Chapter 7

Unpicking the role of reflection and transformative pedagogy for professional education

Introduction

This chapter considers the impact of the pedagogy of initial vocational training for early years practitioners on their understanding of practice and sense of professional identity and status. It explores the role of work-based learning and practice environment in contributing to the development of expertise and the construction of a practice knowledge base. It returns to the issue of developing decisional capital to advance the professionalism of the practitioner, and the importance of critically reflective and transformative pedagogies in supporting this.

Achieving professional recognition

As was noted in the previous chapter, the government, and arguably the early years sector itself, have done little to support the professional status of practitioners. There remains no national career structure and a relatively low-level qualification mandate for registered practice, whilst at the same time, there is a strong externally set regulatory framework and national assessment agenda for young children that holds practitioners to account. Workforce reform over the last 20 years has focused on the development of individual human capital to tackle perceived deficiencies in the quality of practice, through access to qualifications which require the acquisition of a knowledge base arising from approved training content covering child development, curriculum requirements, policy and legislation. Nerland (2018) argues that knowledge as an abstraction is insufficient in defining a workforce as a profession, reinforcing Hargreaves and Fullan's (2012) contention that workforce reform focusing solely on developing the human capital of practitioners would only partially fulfil a professionalisation agenda.

For an occupational group to be recognised as a profession, this requires that individuals demonstrate common practice values and ethics in their work. It also requires that the workforce has autonomy over the content and level of their specialist knowledge base and the capacity to contribute to this knowledge base, as well as autonomy over practice standards qualifications and entry to the workforce (Eraut, 1994; Kinos, 2008; Saks, 2012). This is problematic for the early years workforce (Dyer, 2018), since their qualifications and practice standards, along with their licence to practice, come from the government itself and its regulator (DfE, 2021), as well as from awarding bodies striving to meet government criteria for full and sufficient qualifications, rather than through sector approval. Whilst practitioners themselves, and at organisational

DOI: 10.4324/9780367815387-7

level, their employers, are free to determine the ethical standards and pedagogical choices underpinning their practice, they must still ensure that these choices not only fit legislative requirements but also remain accountable to government and regulators in terms of quality. The early years workforce, therefore, is in a relatively weak position to assert its own professional status and identity.

It is not just a lack of control over their practice and knowledge base that restricts the agency of early years practitioners in making a claim to professional status. Abbott (1988) made the argument that professional status emanates not only from control over practice and its knowledge base, supported by legal controls over the right to licence practice and register members, but also through public recognition and definition of a role, and structures within the workplace to determine the division of labour, set hierarchies and codify job descriptions. Not only does the sector lack the legal control over its workforce, but public understanding and definition of the role of the practitioner are confused, compounded by the overall structure of the sector, where 80% of provision comprises small- and medium-sized PVI organisations, making it so diverse that there is no consensus on job descriptions and terms and condition of service. Public understanding of the practitioner role, as has already been stated, was not helped by the confusing range of qualifications found by the Nutbrown Review (Nutbrown, 2012). It is further undermined by a conflation of the terms 'childcare' and 'nursery education', so that provision can be understood either as a commoditised, babysitting, play-based service for working parents, or as an educational benefit to children, supporting their transition to formal schooling, and offering them the essential foundation skills required for successful literacy and Maths learning. That practitioners describe their roles to parents in naïve and emotionally laden terms further contributes to an understanding of practice as playing with children and keeping them happy, rather than expert-led educational support. Finally, the minimal levels of qualification required for employment, and a hyperfeminised (Osgood, 2010) workforce, as well as the limiting and stereotyped recruitment practices identified by Nutbrown (2012), can all be seen as supporting a view of the practitioner as capable, practical and caring, rather than knowledgeable, critical and expert.

More recent attempts (ONS, 2020) to define the status of the early years practitioner have taken into account the level and length of training required for an individual to be considered competent, and the amount of further experience necessary to support this. The 2020 Standard Occupational Classifications (ONS, 2020) position the more senior, more experienced early years practitioner as an Associate Professional, based on them achieving a Level 3, post-16 qualification, typically over a period of two years, and supplementing this with work experience to develop their practice competence and achieve promotion to leadership roles. This has raised their 'rank' from skilled worker in the previous classification, but without a mandate for graduate practitioners this is as far as the workforce can currently expect to rise in terms of public perception. Since the requirements for Level 3 qualified staff in a setting applies to the minority of staff, there is a growing majority within the workforce whose occupational level will remain as skilled, at best, so that there is no single, consistent level of recognition for workers across the sector. The number and range of different employers, along with no national structure for job descriptions and terms and conditions of service, preclude using the workplace and its hierarchies as a means of asserting the professional status of practitioners, a mechanism available to a wide range of established professions, including the education sector itself.

Professional education and professional status

The question remains, then, of how the early years workforce asserts its professional status and identity. Examination of their habitus (Bourdieu, 1977) and the context of their practice suggest that they are constructed and constrained as occupationally subordinate to schoolteachers, government policy and practice regulators, all of whom exert powerful oversight and control of their practice, and still perceived as subordinate to graduates and other professions. In the context of Hargreaves and Fullan's (2012) analysis of professionalisation, they would seem to lack the infrastructure and autonomy for practice necessary for them to develop social and decisional capital to supplement their apparently increased human capital. Education has long been argued to be the key to increased social capital, and this in turn offers the individual the power and confidence to challenge their existing habitus. But the initial professional education of the practitioner is controlled by the same government bodies that regulate and shape their practice, so that the emphasis of their vocational education is on learning *how to do* rather than considering the whys and wherefores of practice. It is therefore not only the content and level of the initial vocation education of practitioners that serve to perpetuate their restricted capital and autonomy as professionals, but also the pedagogical approach adopted in this training.

The development of expertise in any occupational field would appear to be tied to growing awareness of one's own skill and understanding (Strangaard, 1981; Dreyfus and Dreyfus, 1986; Johns, 2004), and critical reflection at increasingly deeper levels (Goodman, 1984; King and Kitchener, 1994; Schon, 1983). This incrementally empowers the individual not only to broaden their understanding of the knowledge that underpins their practice, but also to question and challenge this knowledge, and use their own experience to generate knowledge of their own. However, the EYFS curriculum framework, the accompanying government-approved practice guidance and the national assessment agenda for children transitioning from the EYFS into Key Stage 1, as discussed in the previous chapter, combine to emphasise the importance of the compliance and accountability of the practitioner. This has resulted in vocational training up to NVQ Level 3 and further professional education for the early years workforce that combines the acquisition of an approved body of knowledge with work-based learning to support its application to practice.

Technicist approaches to professional learning

The Level 3 training courses available to early years practitioners adopt what Schon (1983) has described as a Technical Rationality model of work-based learning. Such an approach encourages the development of set processes and procedures to be followed that are intended to meet the demands of practice typically encountered by the learner. They are based on the assumption that the individual needs and circumstances of practice are always going to be sufficiently similar for such set routines to be applicable, an assumption considered unsafe by Hager (2011), and heavily criticised when applied to early years practice (Moss, 2006; Nutbrown, 2012). This approach, although it includes the consideration of research and theory as a knowledge base, does not necessarily require the learner to analyse how it applies to their own practice or values, but rather to reflect more superficially (Goodman, 1984) on how it has been used to underpin the processes they are required to follow. Hager's (2011) critique of this approach then centres on its construction of work-based learning as a generic, context-free block of learning to be acquired by all learners, and then applied as the practice context requires. Although this offers learners greater security in how to perform their roles, it allows less autonomy in defining them, and much less agency in contributing to the knowledge that underpins their practice and professional development.

Furthermore, accepting the workplace as a site for learning is problematic, not just because of its unpredictability and diversity as a context for developing initial vocational competence, but also in terms of the identity of the learner/practitioner (Boud & Solomon, 2003). Within a technicist understanding of professionalism, especially where the level of necessary technical knowledge is already clearly defined and mandated by regulatory standards, it constructs the novice or apprentice practitioner as less than competent and still learning, and experienced, senior colleagues as competent and in a position to teach or train. Emphasis on individual rather than collective learning, and the acquisition of a body of knowledge or skill, positions the learner or trainee as subordinate to their educators. They are striving to possess rather than own or control the specialist knowledge that underpins their work, instead of being supported to critically reflect on the effectiveness or ethics of established practice. Such a power differential within a workforce can risk undermining the individual development of professional confidence and agency, as the not yet competent consider themselves unable to exercise judgement, and the competent regard professional decision making as their prerogative. Limited access to higher-level work-based qualifications and existing external frameworks to establish practice standards, along with the lack of graduate mandate for leadership roles in practice, serve to reinforce a perception that learning (i.e. the acquisition of knowledge and skills) is a requirement only for those entering the workforce. Once initial vocational training is completed, any reflection on practice is superseded by policy and essential skills updates. Higher-level, more critically reflective professional education at degree level remains available, but only to those practitioners prepared to bear to cost of tuition fee loans themselves from their low-paid employment, and find the time beyond what is often already a very long working week. This effectively discourages more experienced staff from the further professional education required to extend the critical reflection skills that engender a professional identity that incorporates a knowing as well as a doing (Sims-Schouten and Strittrich-Lyons, 2013) self. Only when the workplace is understood as a site for learning at all levels, rather than as an established community of practice (Wenger, 1998) where only novices and apprentices are identified as needing to learn, is this likely to change.

Schon (1983) summed up the shortcomings of the Technical Rationality model as being its focus on problem solving through the selection, from a range of existing options, the best process to meet required ends or outcomes, rather than the development of the skills or knowledge required for 'problem setting' where the student is equipped with skills to 'define the decision to be made' (Schon, 1983, p. 40), i.e. empowered to acquire and use knowledge to make their own judgements about effective practice. Hyland (1997) similarly criticised competence-based education for its behaviourist approach to the development of practice skills and knowledge, arguing that it represented a 'reductionist view of human agency which assumes that knowledge, skills, and values can be codified ... and measured objectively in abstraction from human experience' (Hyland, 1997, p. 495). His argument, that this approach not only oversimplified practice skills but also undermined individual agency, highlights the importance of examining the pedagogy of the training and education practitioners receive. Through such examination, we may come to understand how practitioners are supported in using critical reflection to improve their practice, develop their expertise and establish an understanding of themselves as autonomous professionals.

Developing agency and decisional capital

A pedagogy that emphasises the compliant learning of how things are done rather than the more critical why, or how else they might be done, is one that facilitates the enculturation of a set of practice or professional values that reflect hegemonic discourse and definitions rather than personal values or ethics. The development of a more agentic, critically reflective, self-aware practitioner would appear to require a transformative pedagogy (Mezirow & Taylor, 2009) for their professional education. Such an approach not only offers a deeper understanding of the role of research and the use of theoretical underpinnings to inform practice, but also encourages practitioners to see their experience as a learning opportunity and themselves as contributors to the specialist knowledge base of their work. Using the work of Belenkey et al. (1986), Johns (2004) argues that, by drawing on both their work experience and personal values, along with existing theory and research, reflective practitioners develop their own constructions of knowledge that have ethical and academic credibility. This Voice of Constructed Knowing (Johns, 2004) is what would empower early years practitioners to perceive themselves as creators of knowledge in their field rather than as users of Received Knowledge, becoming what Moss (2006) described as practitioners as researchers rather than technicians.

However, this calls for a learner who is prepared to engage critically with the higher levels of research and theory necessary to support their reflections and evaluations, and who is aware of their own values base and the significance of the ethical implications of care within their practice. In other words, a transformative approach requires a learner who is much more aware of their working environment, at a range of levels, and has the confidence and social capital to engage with it rather than simply accept it. It requires a learner who is comfortable with ambiguity and uncertainty, and confident enough to believe that their own experience and reflections can contribute to the content and definition of the specialist knowledge of their occupational group. It also requires a teacher who understands that *their* role is to encourage dialogue and questioning, rather than requiring the acceptance of received wisdom, supporting the development of the learner's voice from silence to assertion (Johns, 2004). Whilst the student-practitioner has to understand the need for compliance with regulation and legislation, they would seek to achieve this within their own system of values and ethics, personalising rather than standardising their practice, through the process of critical reflection. Such a practitioner would also demonstrate the agency and confidence to question regulatory frameworks and policy decisions, in order to maintain the ethical standards of their practice.

Transformative pedagogy is ultimately empowering but requires that the learner understands and accepts that such an education does not lead to definitive answers about best practice or factual knowledge. Rather, it provides an answer to a situated problem or issue and the tools for readdressing similar situations as they arise in future. Introducing such a personally demanding pedagogy into Level 3 training might seem ambitious, when students are only beginning to learn the fundamentals of supporting children's holistic developmental needs. However, it does not seem unreasonable to introduce elements of transformative pedagogy towards the end of this level of study, particularly as these are the practitioners qualifying to take up leadership roles in the sector. A transformative pedagogy further sets them up with more confidence to engage with higher-level professional education, supporting them more effectively to debate issues concerning children's needs and how best to meet these, and contribute to the knowledge base of their practice.

Understanding competence within transformative education

For a transformative pedagogy to be effective in the field of early years practice, a foundation of skills and knowledge is required, as well as further consideration of the meaning of the term 'competent'. In initial vocational training, this is presented very much as the series of codified skills and behaviours critiqued by Hyland (1997). However, it is important to consider the further connotations of this term, relating to expertise, higher-level knowledge and experience. Illuris (2011) called in to question how the term 'competence' in work-based learning should be understood, challenging its mechanistic and behaviourist connotations. He argued for a broader understanding of the term, moving away from a technicist understanding of the term as simply a repertoire of behavioural responses, to Jorgensen's (1999) definition that it demonstrated a critical understanding of practice:

> It is not merely that a person masters a professional area, but also that the person can apply that professional knowledge – and more than that, apply it in relation to the requirements inherent in a situation which perhaps in addition is uncertain and unpredictable

This definition reflects those incremental understandings of the development of expertise that see the learner moving from received wisdom to the critical application of their own experience-based learning (Strangaard, 1981; Dreyfus and Dreyfus, 1986; Johns, 2004), and presents practice in the workplace as a legitimate tool for generating the knowledge base for professional expertise. Competent practice should not be seen simply as a matter of reproducing set processes and procedures, but of drawing on individual and shared experience to meet the unique circumstances of individual situations. Again, this appears to be a compelling argument for the development of professional education with a transformative pedagogy, based on critical reflection that empowers the learner to articulate their own understanding of practice standards and values and develop decisional capital. Such an approach is based on dialogue, the questioning of how things might otherwise be or be done (Mezirow & Taylor, 2009) and the challenging of taken-for-granted assumptions and values, i.e. the current habitus and doxa of the early years workforce. It could be argued that this approach appears to be a better fit for professional education about practice that has been acknowledged will never be a matter of routine (Nutbrown, 2012), and is a pedagogy associated with undergraduate and postgraduate levels of qualification, where the policy and research considered to underpin practice may be discussed and challenged. It presents learning as a process rather than a product and supports students to consider themselves as entering wider communities of practice that go beyond individual organisations to take in the wider early years sector. This in turn enables them to build the collective voice from the workforce whose absence Hordern (2016) argued is undermining their own claim to professional status.

The workplace as a site for constructing knowledge

The role of the workplace also needs to be reconsidered when exploring pedagogical approaches to professional education and how these impact the identity and status of the early years practitioner. We have already argued that the professional identity of the practitioner has been shaped not only through theory and research into young children's holistic development, but also through the changing context of their practice. Changes to the discourse of early years provision and the accountability of the practitioner to political agenda have also highlighted the need for critical reflection if the early years practitioner is to develop an autonomous professional identity. Illuris (2011) argued that for work-related learning to be effective '[E]veryone must be prepared for their working functions changing constantly and radically during the whole of their working lives' (p. 33). He proposed that this should be addressed through balancing the contributions of the formal classroom and the work setting so that professional education did not simply reflect a narrow focus on current labour market needs, and so that theoretical knowledge could be seen to have its application to practice. The current codifying of vocational qualifications by regulatory and professional bodies as competence statements and occupational frameworks (Reich et al., 2015; Nicolini et al., 2018), which locates the authority to define the knowledge base for practice with educators rather than practitioners, privileges the policymakers and the academic world as the constructors of knowledge to support practice. For early years practitioners to understand themselves as creators of knowledge in their professional field, Nolan and Molla (2018) suggest the academic and practical selves would be better integrated through reframing the relationship between academic study and practice, and bringing the personal, the workplace and the classroom together as equal partners. This offers not only the opportunity to consider the immediate needs of the labour market, but also to develop a broader, critical stance in relation to abstract theory and its application to practice.

Drawing on practice as a means and a context for evaluating and critiquing research, rather than the more orthodox use of theory to drive and justify practice, could more effectively deepen practitioners' critical understanding of theory, and lead to the challenging of established doxa to transform practice, increasing decisional capital. This repositioning of the workplace and the practitioner has the potential to raise the social capital of the workforce and change the public perception of what they do. For the early years sector, this would represent a more democratic approach to work-based learning, as practitioners and employers would be able to determine the skills and knowledge required for good practice on a more equal footing with academics and policymakers. It was seen to offer an effective partnership when sector-endorsed foundation degrees were established, and when the NNEB rather than government approved practitioner qualifications. The more recent control exerted by the DfE over curriculum and practice standards has significantly reduced the voice of the sector in matters of qualifications.

Conclusion

It is the structuring and pedagogic action of the vocational education and professional development opportunities available to early years practitioners that would appear then to significantly influence their professional identity, as well as the level and the content of their training. A Technical Rationality pedagogy, coupled with the traditionally lower entry requirements for early years qualifications, has the effect of reinforcing a vocational habitus, i.e. 'a set of dispositions derived from idealised and realised identities and informed by the notions and guiding ideologies of the vocational culture' (Colley et al., 2003, p. 493) where early years practice 'relies on inherent capacities of women' (Colley, 2006, p. 16), rather than on academic achievement or intellectual capacity. Where these dispositions include a respect for and compliance with hierarchies in return for social and professional approval, rather than critical evaluation of regulation and awareness of the impact of the social and cultural environment of the practitioner, a personal as well as vocational habitus is created where the individual may remain accepting of their lack of power and agency, rather than engaging with the structures around them to challenge their influence. Colley (2006) identifies this in the early years sector as emotional exploitation, where practitioners are expected to sacrifice the potential for greater agency and capital, in return for the satisfaction of doing socially worthy work, for limited financial reward. Such a perception is reinforced by a workforce reform agenda that focuses solely on knowledge acquisition rather than on the increase of decisional and social capital through the development of a national infrastructure for the sector that supports career development.

Bronfenbrenner (1979) argued that the key to an individual's engagement with their environment, and their resulting personal development, lies in their perception of that environment and their own place within it. Opportunities for change to the role and position of the practitioner have included raising their levels of qualification and professional education opportunities, the development of new standards and a framework for practice, and changes to the balance between education and care provision, particularly in the PVI element of the sector. Whilst these might, in theory, offer opportunity for the empowerment and enrichment of the practitioner role, it is how practitioners are educated and supported to engage with these that influence any actual change to the role and identity of the individual. The theoretical frameworks offered by Bourdieu and Bronfenbrenner suggest that practitioners' understanding of their role and professional identity will always be constrained by those who control the curriculum and pedagogy of their professional education. For early years practitioners, there remains a tension between the initial training they must undertake to be licensed as fit and knowledgeable practitioners, and the demands of the role they are then expected to fulfil, with no mandatory requirement for further qualification. They have an initial vocational education that appears to adopt a narrow understanding of competence for its pedagogy, and a practice that is bound by the regulatory and curriculum framework of the EYFS with its accompanying targets and expectations. However, the expectation that they would exercise their own judgement in relation to meeting the needs of individual children suggests that they require a more agentic approach to their professional education, which encourages self-evaluation and the development of personal judgement based on the study of research, the application to practice of theory and practical experience.

Osgood (2010) reported that practitioners found professional education that offered opportunities for developing critical reflection to be most useful to them in developing confidence about their role, and an understanding of how they were positioned within the sector. A transformative approach to professional education, coupled with the development of critical reflection, then, could support practitioners in understanding not only what their vocational habitus (Colley et al., 2003) is, but also how it has developed and how it frames their perceptions of their own professional identity. Such an understanding offers them a base from which to challenge or re-define this. Only by developing deeper skills of critical reflection and recognising the legitimacy of the workplace as a site for generating sector-wide knowledge will they gain the confidence to assert their professional status and identity. However, if the professional education of the practitioner adopts the pedagogic approach described within Schon's model of Technical Rationality (Schon, 1983), then the role of the practitioner is more likely to be one of compliance with regulatory frameworks, where the authors of those frameworks pre-determine appropriate pedagogy and values.

References

Abbott, A. (1988). *The System of Professions: An Essay on the Division of Expert Labour*. London: University of Chicago Press Ltd.

Belenkey, M. F., Clinchy, B. M., Goldberger, N. R. and Tarule, J. M. (1986). *Women's Ways of Knowing: The Development of Self, Voice and Mind*. New York: Basic Books.

Boud, D. and Solomon, N. (2003). "I don't think I am a learner": Acts of naming learners at work. *Journal of Workplace Learning*, 15 (7/8), 326–331. https://doi.org/10.1108/13665620310504800

Bourdieu, P. (1977). *Outline of a Theory of Practice*. Cambridge: Cambridge University Press.

Bronfenbrenner, U. (1979). *The Ecology of Human Development: Experiments by Nature and Design*. Cambridge, MA: Harvard University Press.

Colley, H. (2006). Learning to labour with feeling: Class, gender and emotions in childcare education and training. *Contemporary Issues in Early Childhood*, 7 (1), 15–29.

Colley, H., James, D., Dimont, K. and Tedder, M. (2003). Learning as becoming in vocational education and training: Class, gender and the role of vocational habitus. *Journal of Vocational Education and Training*, 55 (4), 471–498.

DfE (2021). Statutory framework for the early years foundation stage. Crown Copyright: 2021.

Dreyfus, H. L. and Dreyfus, S. E. (1986). *Mind Over Machine: The Power of Human Intuition and Expertise in the Era of the Computer*. Oxford: Blackwell.

Dyer, M. A. (2018). Being a professional or practising professionally. *European Early Childhood Education Research Journal*, 26 (3), 347–361.

Eraut, M. (1994). *Developing Professional Knowledge and Competence*. London: Falmer.

Goodman, J. (1984). Reflection and teacher education: A case study and theoretical analysis. *Interchanges*, 15, 9–26.

Hager, P. (2011). Theories of workplace learning. In: Malloch, M., Cairns, L., Evans, K. and O'Connor, B. N. (eds.), *The Sage Handbook of Workplace Learning*. London: Sage, 17–31.

Hargreaves, A. and Fullan, M. (2012). *Professional Capital: Transforming Teaching in Every School*. London: Routledge.

Hordern, J. (2016). Knowledge, practice and the shaping of early years professionalism. *European Early Childhood and Education Research Journal*, 42 (4), 505–520.

Hyland, T. (1997). Reconsidering competence. *Journal of Philosophy of Education*, 31 (3), 491–503.

Illuris, K. (2011). Workplaces and learning. In Malloch, M., Cairns, L., Evans, K. and O'Connor, B. N. (eds.), *The Sage Handbook of Workplace Learning*. London: Sage, 32–45.

Johns, C. (2004). *Becoming a Reflective Practitioner* (2nd ed.). Oxford: Blackwell Publishing.

Jorgensen, P. S. (1999). Hvad er Kompetence (What is competence?). *Uddannelse*, 9, 4–13.

King, P. M. and Kitchener, K. S. (1994). *Developing Reflective Judgement: Understanding and Promoting Intellectual Growth and Critical Thinking in Adolescents and Adults*. San Francisco: Jossey-Bass Publishers.

Kinos, J. (2008). Professionalism – a breeding ground for struggle. The example of the Finnish day-care centre. *European Early Childhood and Education Research Journal*, 16 (2), 224–241.

Mezirow, J. and Taylor, E. W. (2009). *Transformative Learning in Practice: Insights from Community, Workplace and Higher Education*. San Francisco: Jossey Bass.

Moss, P. (2006). Structure, understandings and discourses: Possibilities for re-envisioning the early childhood worker. *Contemporary Issues in Early Childhood*, 7 (1), 30–41.

Nerland, M. (2018). Knowledge practices and relations in professional education. *Studies in Continuing Education*, 40 (3), 242–256. https://doi.org/10.1080/0158037X.2018.1447919

Nicolini, D., Mørk, B. E., Masovic, J. and Hanseth, O. (2018). The changing nature of expertise: Insights from the case of TAVI. *Studies in Continuing Education*, 40 (3), 306–322. https://doi.org/10.1080/0158037X.2018.1463212

Nolan, A. and Molla, T. (2018). Teacher professional learning through pedagogy of discomfort. *Reflective Practice*, 19 (6), 721–735. https://doi.org/10.1080/14623943.2018.1538961

Nutbrown, C. (2012). *Foundations for Quality: The Independent Review of Early Education and Childcare Qualifications Final Report*. London: Crown Copyright.

Office for National Statistics (ONS) (2020). Standard Occupational Classifications 2020, Volume 1: Structure and descriptions of unit groups. https://www.ons.gov.uk/methodology/classificationsandstandards/standardoccupationalclassificationsoc/soc2020/soc2020volume1structureanddescriptionsofunitgroups#summary-of-the-changes-to-the-classification-structure-introduced-in-soc-2020

Osgood, J. (2010). Reconstructing professionalism in ECEC: The case for the 'critically reflective emotional professional'. *Early Years*, 30 (2), 119–133.

Reich, A., Rooney, D. and Boud, D. (2015). Dilemmas in continuing professional learning: Learning inscribed in frameworks or elicited from practice. *Studies in Continuing Education*, 37 (2), 131–141. https://doi.org/10.1080/0158037X.2015.1022717

Saks, M. (2012). Defining a profession: The role of knowledge and expertise. *Professions and Professionalism*, 2 (1), 1–10.

Schon, D. (1983). *The Reflective Practitioner: How Professionals Think in Action*. Aldershot: Ashgate Publishing.

Sims-Schouten, W. and Strittrich-Lyons, H. (2013). 'Talking the talk': Practical and academic self-concepts of early years practitioners in England. *Journal of Vocational Education and Training*, 66 (1), 39–55.

Strangaard, F. (1981). *NLP Made Visual*. Copenhagen: Connector.

Wenger, E. (1998). *Communities of Practice: Learning, Meaning and Identity*. New York: Cambridge University Press.

Chapter 8

Empowerment and agency
Reflections on narratives of practice

Introduction

In this final chapter we draw further on data from our own studies to consider how practitioners negotiate and construct their professional identities as they achieve graduate-level qualifications. The pen portraits, monologues and vignettes selected illustrate the connection between professionalism and leadership and provide examples both of the empowerment and the restrictions associated with professionalisation of the ECEC workforce. The chapter concludes by considering, overall, how professionalisation of a workforce, considered so essential in ensuring children's safeguarding and well-being and in securing their readiness for formal education, can be advanced not only for them, but also by them.

Leadership and the early years practitioner: McMahon (2016)

For the first layer of analysis in my doctoral study (McMahon, 2016) I presented extended narratives or monologues from the participants own words, and pen portraits that give some background information about individual participant practitioners. Lauren, who worked in a private pre-school setting, did not deny the effects of underfunding and lack of graduate salary on becoming a professional and she did ultimately leave the PVI sector to become a teacher in a Reception class. Nevertheless, her monologue highlights the interplay between professionalism and leadership and contains constructive and practical lessons for setting managers/owners and future graduate professionals.

Lauren pen portrait

Lauren works in a private pre-school which is owned by her aunt, and has done since leaving school after her A levels. When Lauren was younger, her aunt and her daughter, Lauren's cousin, lived with Lauren and her family for a time, and Lauren has a close relationship with her aunt. Lauren completed her NVQ Level 3 at the pre-school and her job title is Pre-School Assistant. Although she has only worked at one setting, Lauren has undertaken a placement at an additional setting to gain experience in the baby room. At her own setting, Lauren has responsibility for 14 key children aged between three and five years, and, although she describes herself as ambitious, she cannot imagine herself working as a manager in the office. After completing her Level 3, Lauren enrolled on the foundation degree at the university, where we met, and then decided to progress onto EYPS. After achieving EYPS, Lauren was keen to complete the BA (Hons) Early Years so that she can then qualify to work in a school as a Reception teacher.

DOI: 10.4324/9780367815387-8

Lauren monologue

I can't remember, well nothing specific, that I wanted to do at school. You know when they ask you, what do you want to be? One day I wanted to be a vet, the next a hairdresser but I always loved children. I was always surrounded by children, having younger siblings, and mum was a childminder. I used to babysit and was interested in children. But at school you were channelled into sixth form, and it was all about A levels and going to university. I chose my options, nothing to do with what I do now, Psychology, Textiles … can't remember … oh, and Biology. In Year 10 I went into a school for my work experience, and I loved it and wanted to be a Reception teacher, but I was no good at exams and it was all about university. I didn't get the grades. NVQ would have been better for me, but we didn't get any advice. I think my aunty has been really important. She gave me that chance, she took a chance, gave me a job in the pre-school after my A levels when I thought what will I do now? After A levels, I was down-hearted, but the foundation degree turned that round a bit and to be honest I think I'm better off than those doing full time uni. I'll have five years' experience and the grades. I did want to move out and live with friends, but this has so worked out best for me.

EYPS is the next step up. I want to move on and up. I'm in a private family pre-school and I will have to move on. EYPS will move me on. That is what I need, more of a challenge. I've been there since leaving school and, as they have an EYP, there's not so much I can bring to the table. I'm lucky to have support in my setting; they are really pushing me. The EYP has already highlighted about seven things on her job description for me to do, and I'm leading all the planning meetings now. I've heard from some of the others how they struggle to get time off to attend EYPS days. I'm lucky the pre-school leader is an EYP. Level 3s have not really heard of it or understand it. Some people come into childcare as a last resort and it's not a passion. Some people are not in the right job position; they have the title manager because they have been there long-est, but they are not doing what's on the badge. Things are stricter now you have to have English and Maths and EYTS or EYPS to be in with the children, that means they get the direct benefit, but managers need skills and training. Managers do not have to be hands on, but they need training. EYT is really good because it's an incentive to work for it. It's the right to be here, and it will bring a lot more people into early years rather than just primary and secondary. The EYT will know about play and can implement it better than some of the others and because of their leadership they will be able to get it across to staff, so that it won't be too formal. It's definitely a good thing.

I think when you are young you are not seen as professional at work; you're just there with the kids. Some people walk in and see you as a student or a volunteer, whereas you've been there five years and I'm quite experienced for my age. So, when you get this status people will think, she s got the degree and done the work. It gives you a lot more self-worth and confidence. I think a lot of people look at you and think you've not done very well at school, so you've gone into childcare, just there to babysit. Whereas, actu-ally, I've done all this work and we're not just here to look after the children but to educate them. I hated school. My first day at primary, the childminder said they had to peel me off her. I want to give children a nicer experience than I had. Teachers never liked me. I was a day dreamer, I was bullied, and secondary school was worse. With the bullying and everything, I'm interested in that. Even from three years old, children have friendship groups. Working with three- to five-year-olds, you get to see the impact you have on them; you can see how much they change. Through this, I grow as a person.

Before the parents wouldn't t come to me but now, I do one to one with a child and his mum always comes over and asks for advice. A lot of the parents have been asking me how I've been doing at university. It's all about confidence. I've never liked conflict but now I'm able to talk to them, the staff, rather than make it a big deal. It's a confidence thing. Because you are working towards something, you put all your effort and hard work into it so you kind of deserve... you have value, what you do is valued.

The process gives you more self-worth; it's definitely boosted my confidence. At work, they know me but in the other setting they don't know me. It just comes across as me being like that. It's easier to be like that, seen as more of a professional. Whereas in my setting, I've been there since sixth form and they've known me as a student, from going through the Foundation Degree up to now. If I start trying to delegate where they know you, they look at you as if you don't normally do that. In placement, you are really going in as a student and you have to ask permission to do stuff. In your own setting, they know what you are doing, and they understand the process. In placement, you have to say, 'Is it alright if I do this?' You have to be a leader but don't want to come across as taking over. When the other EYP was doing it, some of the staff said, 'We didn't know that you were so self-centred, saying I did this about everything,' but now they know it's not so self- absorbed. You have to lead staff, it builds your confidence, and you have to negotiate and talk to higher management, ask them, and explain things. You have to explain to staff in the room, so I think it helps them understand why you are doing it. It's all about leadership. If you are going to be an early years professional, you have to lead, and this is one of the big parts of doing it.

It's been hard, not in terms of, you know, you are doing it every day but it's a lot of paperwork, so it's testing your organisational skills. It's been time consuming, definitely, with working at the same time and, if I was to do it again, I wouldn't have left the documentary evidence folder to the last minute. My mum s been there as I've been sat at the computer, bringing tea, endless amounts of tea. The manager and room leader have done it themselves and they've been there to support me, to know that they've done it and you can see their leadership skills, they've mentored me. It's definitely been helpful having them there as opposed to someone like Karen who's not had anyone there who knows the process; it's been more of a challenge to get anyone to understand why she's doing things.

The setting visit, I think it went well. I was rather nervous but not as daunting as I thought. She [the assessor] came and observed my activity and she commented on how good it was, which was good. They really enjoyed it, so I was quite glad. I went down for the interview, and she only had three questions. Obviously because I'd not been in a baby room until this year, she had a few questions about the babies. It's a bit nerve-wracking being put on the spot but I could answer them all and I'd tried to cover everything three times in the evidence folder and then cover them again on the tour. I'm relieved it's all over, but I felt positive. It's definitely been worth it. I'm in limbo but I understand the process and I've done everything I can so that s okay.

Fingers crossed I've passed. I'm hoping to stay at my setting until I've done the Honours degree but unfortunately our hours have been cut at work. So, when we go back in September, we'll be down five hours. Our contracts were changed last year to be flexible, but they may have to let a member of staff go, and at the moment it's between me and her. So, if I've got my EYP, hopefully, then it gives me a bit more security. It's not good but I'm hoping that once I get my status it will give me an advantage. There's no hope of a graduate salary, it's very hard, so we'll see. I don't want to go into managing a setting; I've done this to be in the room with the children. I've always wanted to go into Reception; there's more security in a school than a private or charity run business. So, once I've got my EYP status and honours, obviously going into a school you're going up against people who have done a four-year university course, but I've always thought that, if I'm going up against them, I've got five years' experience, whereas they've got placement. I know that's experience but it's not the same, whereas you've been there, working with parents, you've been doing learning journeys for five years and you know the EYFS. I hope it will give me an advantage. Well, if not, it will level me out. You probably will have to argue your point because a lot of people won't recognise it, but the status adds to it and the more people who do it, the more recognised it will become. EYT will really add to it. People will become more aware of it, hopefully.

Lauren draws attention to the role of mentoring and support from the senior management team in her progress towards graduate status. In Lauren's setting, leadership appeared to be understood as a communal concept (Siraj and Hallet, 2014) whereby all could be engaged in it, and this was endorsed by the setting manager. The setting manager and deputy were graduate professionals, suggesting that the setting was a learning-centred community, which Hallet (2014) argues is essential for pedagogical leaders to learn together through reflection and discussion. The OECD (2021) also highlight the important role leaders play in supporting professional development initiatives, and this was central to Lauren's success.

She also speaks of her increased confidence and how this has enabled her to work more effectively with parents and colleagues. Arguably her increased levels of confidence characterise a release of personal agency as described by McDowall Clark and Murray (2012) as part of a model of leadership from within, rather than one linked to a position of authority. Confidence matters because, as Davis (2014, p. 159) identified, it is the 'boosting *force which triggers action for change, giving authority to use existing knowledge*' and it appears that for Lauren, her increasing levels of confidence were central to her taking on a leadership role. Practitioner confidence is influenced by a complex interplay of factors and is integral to professional identity, as discussed in Chapters 2 and 3. In the monologue Lauren states her passion for working with young children, and this is described as a key driver of ECEC leader's practice (Hallet, 2014).

Lauren went on to identify some key leadership skills she used such as negotiating and getting the balance right between working collaboratively and not taking over. Finally, she demonstrated her willingness to reflect honestly on her experiences and hoped that by participating in the study more people would get to know about graduate professional status and be attracted into the sector. This narrative simultaneously illustrates the enormous positive effect for the individual of becoming a graduate professional and how this becomes a loss for the ECEC sector. It provides a stark reminder of how the lack of a clearly defined career pathway with commensurate pay and conditions deprives the PVI sector of highly qualified graduate professional leaders.

Personal agency and identity: Dyer (2018)

This research focused on how early years practitioners constructed and articulated their professional identity, what it meant to them to be an early years practitioner. The study included 23 semi-structured interviews with practitioners working across the early years sector in a range of organisations, using the Listening Guide (Mauthner and Doucet, 1998; Doucet and Mauthner, 2008) to interpret what these practitioners said.

This data analysis tool was developed to explore narrative data for its plot – the stories individuals tell about themselves – and for the relationships each individual narrator focuses on. Since the study took its theoretical framework for the construction of identity from work that foregrounded power relationships and the interactions that these permitted or promoted, it made sense to use an analysis tool that focused on self-construction within the context of collegial, professional and hierarchical relationships. The Listening Guide encourages the researcher to use up to three different readings of data to arrive at a 'constructed self', i.e. an understanding, through the content of their narratives and the relationships they discuss, of how an individual creates their identity. From these readings, it was then possible and plausible to create vignettes from the experiences they shared of their practice and their values. Four of these stories are set out below, each with its own tale to tell about the tensions and conflicts over practice values, perceived status and professionalism that these practitioners often face, as well as the sense of empowerment they have gained from higher-level professional education.

Florence

Florence worked as a nursery nurse in a school-based nursery class, with responsibility for supporting children's learning and development and their preparation for transition to Reception class in school. The school itself was attached to a Children's Centre with full day care provision for children up to the age of five, but this provision was managed separately from the school's own nursery class.

There is a routine set out. We do have a timetable but given the environment, that can waiver depending where you've had accidents or upsets but the rule of thumb is Register half past 8 while about 20 to 9, free play, in between that there are structured group activities, and then we have an organised tidy up time, then back to the planned/free play, then story and then more or less home time and in between that we have music sessions and PE ... For me, it's [my priority] so they feel safe, so they feel secure, they're settled, they're comfortable and then all of that follows. But policy wise we have to do the phonics and we have to do the literacy and we have to do maths, and honestly some are not ready when they come in to do that even after a term, they're not ready. If they come from a stressful environment and you're wanting highly structured activity, you're not going to get it if they've not done their own little bit in play first. It's just finding that balance and sometimes it's really difficult when you've got assessments and targets to meet from the profile...

If we'd not had the timetable, that little boy's telescope that he'd made, his learning could have been built on and we could have gone back to it but because of the timetable and the routine that had to stop because of the other accidents. So maybe more flexibility that way but we do have to have a timetable ... Yes, we need a routine, but I don't think it has to be structured as such, that play or development is cut short because we have to tidy because we have to do PE, or we have to go down to the hall to sing, or we have to do the structured group work, maybe that could come in between doing other things. You can do your 3D solids, shapes while you've got your junk modelling, and do it that way and you've still got to have your tick list, but you could still tick them off. You could do it outside, inside but you know, we have to have a timetable.

You see Day Care is structured differently to your school setting and even though we have wrap around care from Day Care into school, I think that, well the Day Care provision that we've got at school, the people work with and put their needs first, the children... It's different because they've got babies right up to 3, 4, and their structure is more flexible. They [the children] take their shoes and their socks off in there, you know, they run round, and then they come into nursery, and they take their own shoes and socks off so ... and it will cause a bit of a discrepancy sometime because our practice as such is you keep your shoes and socks on in nursery.

it's [management of practice] top down and you're actually on the front line and you're dealing with little people and it's totally different to reading it from a book or from a sheet, and you're tuned in to how their behaviour and try and think on their level, and you know them and you're spending 3 and half hours every day, you do get to know little snippets and I think reading things from a policy or a book just sometimes doesn't work.

Florence is clearly frustrated with the management of practice that appears to prioritise routine and structure to offer children some stability, rather than taking a more child-led approach that prioritises children's individual needs and interests. However, the language and tone of her narrative undermine her challenge for a different approach to practice. She sets out her argument in language that reflects a more practical than academic self (Sims-Schouten and Strittrich-Lyons, 2013), using the typically unsophisticated language reported by Brownlee et al. (2000) and Berthelsen and Brownlee (2007), presenting her own values and ethics as being in opposition to more powerful policy and procedural requirements. Despite graduating with a first-class honours degree, she lacks the professional confidence or status to challenge the existing hierarchy or to advocate for a change to setting practice. Her argument is based on her own experience and understanding of what is best for young children's holistic development rather than drawing on the research and theory she has so successfully engaged with throughout her studies. With her degree qualification, based on critical reflection of practice, policy and research, she represents the graduate leader of practice that was sought to raise standards in the early years sector. However, with no career progression pathway – she retains the 'nursery nurse' role she was initially employed as with her NVQ Level 3 qualification – she has no additional decisional or social capital, no elevated status or recognition to support her in driving change based on this higher level of understanding. Autonomy and agency are missing from her narrative and from her role within the school. To address this, she will have to pursue qualified teacher status (her ultimate ambition) and change her role, which will serve to increase her status and social capital, but which means she takes on a different role and becomes something else. Such a solution to the lack of autonomy of the practitioner does not advance the cause of the workforce collectively and raises issues about the kind of practitioner or professional they want to be.

Rose

Rose worked in a primary school, offering teaching and learning support to the youngest children and often working with children whose behaviour in class is quite challenging. She took a very principled approach to her practice, considering the individual needs of the children and advocating for their autonomy and choice in their play, an approach reflecting an affective and compassionate understanding of pedagogy (Taggart, 2014). She was particularly worried about the imposition of apparently arbitrary rules over children's play, and a strong focus on the achievement of assessment targets that did not take into account the developmental needs of very young learners.

It's very rare you get time to just be free to be with the children and get involved in the play and things like that. It's usually an activity focus or you're outside supporting play outside. So it's difficult because I know from what I've learnt at Uni how I should be towards the children but how I see myself towards them is basically realistically getting the things done as are in the timetable ... you'll lead the activity at the table and they can choose to come to you or a new role play is set out you'll be timetabled to play with the role play with the children and to encourage them to use it properly ... rather than run round playing drums with the cauldron which they might like to do, we have to kind of try and direct the play to the focus as it's intended ... They're only allowed to wear their dressing up shoes for inside, they're not allowed to then go outside ... I would love to let them do that ...it's part of how they learn, how they develop, and they could be engaged ... sometimes it's so sad to make them take things off before they go outside because they might have dressed up in something inside and they're building their own role play in their home corner and then they want to take it outside and continue it and then you've got to stop them and say 'No take that off, that stays inside'

.... Sometimes people forget they're little people and self-esteem and things like that and they don't realise how you speak to them, your body language, if you're approachable, but I'm very much that way inclined so that's why I get so frustrated when people don't have that ... What I hate to see is in a numeracy lesson with a clear objective and it keeps getting banged on and banged on regardless of what the children are doing, they've lost interest, they've had enough, they're rolling about on the carpet and they're getting screamed at because they have to finish this lesson, they have to understand. ... And I look at them and they're struggling to sit on the carpet. Or some of them especially with some boys we've got, 'I can't write'.... 'Why can't you ...' and they just can't write, they're just not ready to write ... children are expected to do something at a chronological age because the EYFS says 'they should be able to do this within this month bracket' and I get so frustrated when they're told, 'Right you have to do this and you have to write something' and the child hasn't got the motor skills that come before it and although an intervention might be put in place ... there's still no let up and then how Practitioners might deal with that child who can't do their writing and how much it's hammered home. But I think if you had a knowledge [of child development] ....But then even if you have a knowledge, you've got to be free to use it, I suppose, which is a challenge, but some people just don't .... I don't think they've got a holistic view of the child and it frustrates me.

after I've done my 'Top Up' I want to do teacher training, but I don't know if I could work within the mainstream school because I'm scared of getting that [my own values] taken out of me and getting in the mundane targets, Ofsted, assessments and I'm questioning whether I can do that. I really don't know where I want to go, I'm confused at the moment because I'm so worried about losing how I feel.

This last statement sums up Rose's overriding concern – that a more formal education role as a teacher might expose her to the overwhelming pressures of a target led, outcome-driven approach to practice, something she feels to be at odds with her own principles for ethical practice. Her narrative is an impassioned argument for the recognition of children's rights, and in particular their right to play, and an approach to practice based on compassion and empathy. However, like Florence, Rose, who also graduated with a first-class honours degree, still felt she lacked the status or professional credibility to challenge her colleagues' lack of knowledge about young children's learning or development, or a leadership of practice that sets arbitrary rules that impedes on children's play-based learning. Higher-level qualifications would appear to be insufficient on their own to give practitioners the confidence to see themselves as agentic professionals – infrastructure and the wider recognition that Abbot (1988) describes as jurisdictions are also required.

Claire

Claire, like Florence and Rose, also worked in a primary school, supporting children's learning and development in Reception class. Her narrative was particularly striking when she discussed the value of having a degree-level qualification, both to her practice and to her remuneration. She valued the knowledge her Foundation degree gave her, and the way it has prepared her to engage with her honours-level studies. However, she still placed a premium on experience, an emphasis on the practical aspects of early years practice rather than the theoretical or intellectual, echoing research findings of Sims-Schouten and Strittrich-Lyons (2013). In her whole narrative she spoke at length about having the time and empathy to discuss individual children's needs and progress with their parents, drawing on her own experience as a parent. However, when discussing her level of qualification, she was somewhat ambivalent about whether this should be recognised, either in terms of salary or simply in terms of being recognised as a higher level of knowledge.

I have got a foundation degree. At school not many people know I have got that, and as far as work's concerned it does not come with any more responsibilities, I do the job that I do, whether I have got the foundation degree or not ... parents don't know that I have the foundation degree and ... they [the other nursery nurses] have level 3 which is the requirement of being a nursery nurse, so parents know that's the level, they don't know the difference between us, we are all across the board the same. Which to be fair, I agree with ... to me, [if] you go and do a job that requires a set of skills and if you choose to go and educate yourself further, then yes, it should be acknowledged but not in the payroll sense, ... it was my choice to be a nursery nurse, ... if that is the level that society sees it requires, then that is what I should be paid as, and if they want more... from me with an early years degree, then that is the education [authority's] job to decide whether they want that from me. Or I could go on and get a different job myself ... we are doing the same job and we're all there for the children it was my choice to go educate myself further. Yes, the knowledge I have got from this degree has been immense and staff at work know I have that knowledge and they can see it but for me a lot of early years is practice ... I have been in this school setting for 10 years before I came back to study, I wouldn't have engaged in this course as much and as well I think if I hadn't had that 10 years' experience. Childcare is a lot about experience.

For Claire, it would appear that having a degree is a valuable personal achievement rather than a professional one that will raise her status. The crux of her argument focuses on the infrastructure of the sector – her job role has not changed, and she was not required to gain this additional knowledge or qualification, so why would she expect greater remuneration or recognition. In Foucauldian terms (Foucault (1982), cited in Rabinow (1984)), the 'scientific classification' of her role, despite her own increase in knowledge, has not altered; therefore, her own expectations should not change, demonstrating the power of existing structures and perceptions to influence how we see ourselves, and the risk this poses of exploitation for her personal and emotional commitment to her role (Colley, 2006; Taggart, 2011). She represents a clear example of the limitations of a professionalisation agenda that focuses solely on human capital, without the development of social or decisional capital (Hargreaves and Fullan, 2012), and without a clear jurisdiction (Abbot, 1988) for professional status. What Claire lacks is the agency or power to argue for greater recognition, limiting her status if she wants to remain in her current job role.

Iris

Iris had a management role within a private day care setting attached to a primary school in an area suffering from significant socio-economic deprivation. She had just graduated with a first-class honours degree in Early Years, and spent the five years she studied for this applying her growing understanding of theory to practice within her setting. The organisation she worked in had a clear hierarchy of staff posts, giving Iris opportunity to progress in her career, taking on additional responsibilities and developing confidence in her own judgement and leadership. She spoke of what she had done, and her awareness of her position as a role model for newer staff.

I'm in charge of all the education side of things in the Day Care ... I think you've got to have a very good knowledge of children's development and understanding what their next steps need to be, it's a very big part of the EYFS and something that we always try to ensure we incorporate in children's observations. That it's not just observing them and comparing them to the EYFS and meeting where they are but also where they need to be so also ensure that there's next steps to put on... If you're aware of what a child should be achieving, then ... you can always plan for their next steps then. I think it's important, especially as a senior to have understanding of ... team work and being able to have good relationships with your staff so they understand where you want, what your expectations are, not just for the children but on a professional level ... we would expect that a senior practitioner show the same professionalism as what I do ... there is good language between the practitioner and the child, good language between the practitioner and the parent, paper work is done to a higher level, there's a good understanding of the Nursery Policies, EYFS. If a parent asks a question, then that practitioner is able to give them a professional answer that is jargon free and the parents can understand it you need to be a strong character especially if you're wanting to be a senior ... I've got a very good team around me but you do need to be strong because if there's something that you would want to put in action or something that you need to change, you need to be able to address that and do it in a professional way which staff will respond to and take immediate action. But I think you need to be happy ... Because children need a happy environment to learn.

We have free play opportunities for children so they access indoors and outdoors on a daily basis so children are learning through their own play but the practitioners that we've got are very highly qualified and are working toward being highly qualified, so they can provide things ... when I was learning at University I implemented things such as the sustained shared thinking with staff, making sure that all staff were aware of what it meant and how we could actually put it into play practice.

Not trying not to be a bit big headed but I can see the Nursery has developed immensely ... especially since I achieved my EYPS, but throughout my journey, from foundation degree to my BA Honours, EYPS status, I've grown in confidence which has had a rippling effect on the practitioners that I work alongside. They ask much more questions than what they did initially, they're wanting to learn more; there's actually a member of staff now who is going to university and starting her BA Honours in Early Years in September because she's wanting to be a Deputy Manager, so I'd like to think that I've inspired her to further her professional development as well. But I definitely think it's made a big difference and impact on the setting, ... the area of this school is highly deprived, and I do think I've made a big impact because I'm aware of children's needs now a bit more that what I was when I started. I can kind of think of things to put into practice as opposed to what I used to be like when I first started, and I think that's happened through confidence and my own experience ... but I do definitely think the degree has made a huge impact on that.

The room that I currently work in is a 2 – 4 so there's quite a big difference in children's development so the planning document that I produced covers ever child's age but also allows me to plan for their individual learning as well through good communication with staff and activities that are easily differentiated for each child's needs. Again the degree has influenced and increased my knowledge of the EYFS so I'm now able to know the ins and outs of the EYFS and what is expected not just 'right this is what communication means, this is what maths means', but actually I understand the guidelines and framework of the EYFS and why it's there and what we're doing things for as opposed to 'We've got to do it for EYFS'. ... and I think that's helped in producing things like the planning document and just on a general daily basis.

I've been appointed Behaviour Manager in the early years foundation stage, which includes Day Care Nursery and Reception. And basically, I put guidelines in; I'm saying guidelines because everyone is different, and some children need different targets and strategies ... So, we do have the Thinking Chair, we do sit with that child while they think about what they may have done ... that's the strategy that I've implemented and it's currently working. But we've had some children that have come through and those strategies don't work for them, so I had to research different strategies that may have worked for them in a different way and then put them in practice.

I think one of the main things for me in particular was confidence and the degree gave me a lot of confidence and ... one apprentice, she's absolutely amazing but she doesn't see how good she is because she's got low confidence. So, my job is seeing her, I don't need to tell her anything because she knows, ... she just needs to start believing in herself now.

Iris's narrative is one of empowerment, detailing the many positive aspects of degree-level study, and how this has enhanced her practice. Her narrative stresses her sense of commitment, to the children and families she works with, and also to her colleagues, a relational and interpersonal approach to professional identity that has been identified by early years researchers (Oberhuemer, 2005; Page, 2017, 2018). There is little evidence here of the frustration or anxiety experienced by Florence and Rose, and none of the ambivalence to her qualification shown by Claire. Iris makes it clear that it is the combination of her knowledge, her critical understanding of how theory underpins practice and her personal disposition and affective connection with the children that ensures her practice is good. However, whilst she has had opportunity, through working in this particular organisation, to rise up the hierarchy and take on more responsibility, any further career development requires that she now needs to change career pathway if she wants to remain working directly with the children. Bordieusian analysis would suggest that Iris has gained the capital and agency to change her own habitus, but rather than challenging her current 'structured structures' (Bourdieu, 1977, p. 72), she is moving beyond them. Since this interview, Iris has gone on to train as a primary school teacher, still working with the children she values so highly, but in a different role with its own established habitus and status.

Conclusion

The narratives included in this chapter illustrate the diversity of the individual experience of becoming a professional which in turn reflects the complexity of professionalisation of the ECEC workforce. Each experience was shaped by the individual's beliefs and principles, organisational culture and wider external policy drivers including qualifications and occupational standards. These are constructed on deeply embedded inequities associated with class, gender and the divide between education and care and reflect multiple contradictions at the heart of ECEC (Chapter 1), and the original conception of the graduate professional (Chapter 2). In summary, the graduate professional is conceived as technician complying with externally imposed standards, yet simultaneously required and expected to be an autonomous, reflective change agent. Professionalisation and leadership have been conflated and closely linked to the improvement agenda, yet there is little training for leadership. For the individual practitioner, qualifications can be transformative in terms of practice, professional development and identity. Ironically, however, this can mean they then leave the sector, so that perversely, the current approach to professionalisation is depleting the sector of highly qualified graduate professionals.

The professionalisation agenda for the early years workforce stands now at a critical juncture, balancing the raising of professional status and agency with the retention of highly qualified practitioners in early years settings, most particularly within the PVI sector. Progress has been made through the introduction of higher-level qualifications, but any headway gained now appears under threat due to unresolved issues of lack of career structure, low pay and low status. Having addressed the apparent knowledge deficit identified by early workforce reform consultations (DfES, 2005, 2006), attention needs to turn to ways of developing greater decisional and social capital. Throughout this book, there is repeated mention of infrastructure and career pathway, but these remain problematic. Abbot (1988) argued that it is jurisdictions and vacancies that give support to professional status, but this requires a consensus across the individual settings and nursery chains across the sector, and is more likely to be achieved through a regulatory framework, i.e. a return to a regulatory expectation of graduate leadership for practice, underpinned by mandate. Such an expectation will only be achieved when both the regulating authority and government recognise the level of skills and critical understanding required by the role they expect practitioners to fulfil.

Graduate practitioners currently have little incentive to remain in early years settings, and those that do, do so at the expense of graduate remuneration and recognition, perpetuating an exploitative vocational habitus (Colley, 2006; Colley et al., 2003) that privileges personal commitment, experience, and interpersonal skills over academic achievement and critical reflection. A clearer infrastructure that applies to all settings would at least make explicit the worth of the graduate in early years practice, and would give them the status and responsibility they currently lack and seem reluctant to claim for themselves. Acknowledgement that senior staff have the critical reflection skills, and deeper knowledge of young children's development and learning, could reasonably lead to an expectation that they take responsibility for steering and leading practice and quality improvement, rather than relying on a framework of apparently universal practice techniques and developmental outcomes to guarantee quality. However, such acknowledgement, whilst increasing the scope for the development of decisional capital and autonomy within the individual workplace, might weaken the authority of the external regulator, changing the balance of some power relationships within the sector. Evetts (2011) argues that professionalisation 'from above' is actually a means of controlling and regulating practice, so such an empowering move may not prove popular with external bodies trying to shape and steer the role of the practitioner.

Whilst the introduction of career infrastructure would support the development of decisional capital, the workforce also needs increased social capital. What is missing from the narratives shared here is the autonomous and agentic voice of constructed knowing (Johns, 2004), used to articulate not only values and ethics but also knowledge distilled from experience and critical reflection. A more transformative pedagogy for their professional education would support practitioners to engage with and challenge current power relationships, and develop the confidence they need to assert their values in practice and pedagogic leadership. It further supports them in understanding themselves as constructors as well as receivers of knowledge, supporting the development of a practice knowledge base from within the sector, a factor regarded as key when defining professionalism (Brock, 2012; Lloyd and Hallet, 2010; Dalli, 2008; Eraut, 1994). Finally, transformative professional education at graduate level could set up partnerships between practitioners and universities bringing the workplace and the research community together to give credibility and status to this knowledge base.

However, although relationships with HEIs and greater recognition for knowledge gained though experience can contribute to raising the status of the early years practitioner and their work, the workforce needs to act and operate as a sector rather than as individual staff teams – their community of practice needs to extend beyond the setting. Hordern (2016) identified a lack of collectivity that was holding practitioners back from laying claim to their own knowledge base, or challenging established authorities and doxa of practice. Prior to this, Lumsden (2012) argued the need for professional socialisation, her research identifying networking groups as vital in sharing and developing practice knowledge across early years settings. Opportunities for networking at local level were once provided through Sure Start units and EYDCP teams, but austerity cuts have drastically reduced these. National opportunities still exist both in person and online, but may be costly and daunting for the individual practitioner. Furthermore, there remains the issue of practitioners having the confidence to perceive themselves as being allowed to express their voice in a wider community of practice, or to have a point of view about practice that is worth sharing. They need to understand themselves as experts with skills and knowledge to contribute, and that this networking is as much a vital element in their ongoing CPD, as First Aid and child protection updates; that their practice and pedagogical leadership are not just about compliance with regulatory framework but will only develop and improve through shared debate and critical reflection.

Opportunities for networking and the sharing of practice therefore need to be made available for practitioners by practitioners, but this process remains a difficult one to start for a fragmented workforce that continues to be presented, and even to perceive itself, as subordinate to other professional groups. Social media platforms have more recently been seen to be effective in mobilising the sharing of opinions and ideas, but often these have been ad hoc and reactive responses to issues that impact practice, rather than more systematic and proactive critical reflection to construct a shared knowledge base. How, then, can the workforce be supported in its professionalisation from within?

At present the workforce struggles to construct itself as a profession, within the current understanding of what this term means. Their knowledge base is multidisciplinary and controlled by those who set the terms for their vocational education and licence to practice. There are no required standards for the leadership of practice. These factors combine to reduce the decisional and social capital of practitioners, encouraging them in a vocational habitus of compliance rather than autonomy. We would therefore argue that a new, more relational and democratic understanding of professionalism (Oberhuemer, 2005), that privileges the so-called soft skills of interpersonal communication, team working and collegiality, is required to empower practitioners to value what they bring to their practice and leadership. They need to understand that it is not just their knowledge – once in deficit but now greatly improved – but also the way they apply this knowledge that makes them the unique professional that they are. We would argue for a more transformative approach to the pedagogy of their professional education, to be able to challenge policy and practice with confidence and authority, in support of a quality improvement agenda based on the needs of the child. We would further reiterate our argument for a graduate mandate, particularly for the leaders of practice, and for leadership standards that encourage critical reflection and self-evaluation. Most importantly, we would argue for a career and sector infrastructure that recognises the value of a graduate-led, highly qualified workforce, so that those seeking appropriate recognition for their professionalism no longer feel that they need to become something other than an early years practitioner to achieve this.

References

Abbot, A. (1988). *The System of Professions: An Essay on the Division of Expert Labour.* London: University of Chicago Press Ltd.

Berthelsen, D. and Brownlee, J. (2007). Working with toddlers in child care: Practitioners' beliefs about their role. *Early Childhood Research Quarterly*, 22, 347–362.

Bourdieu, P. (1977). *Outline of a Theory of Practice.* Cambridge: Cambridge University Press.

Brock, A. (2012). Building a model of early years professionalism from practitioners' perspectives. *Journal of Early Childhood Research*, 11 (1), 27–44.

Brownlee, J., Berthelsen, D., Boulton-Lewis, G. and McCrindle, A. (2000). Caregivers beliefs about practice in infant childcare programmes. *International Journal of Early Years Education*, 8 (2), 155–165.

Colley, H. (2006). Learning to labour with feeling: Class, gender and emotions in childcare education and training. *Contemporary Issues in Early Childhood*, 7 (1), 15–29.

Colley, H., James, D., Dimont, K. and Tedder, M. (2003). Learning as becoming in vocational education and training: Class, gender and the role of vocational habitus. *Journal of Vocational Education and Training*, 55 (4), 471–498.

Dalli, C. (2008). Pedagogy, knowledge and collaboration: Towards a ground up perspective on professionalism. *European Early Childhood Education Research Journal*, 16 (2), 171–185.

Davis, G. (2014). Graduate leaders in early childhood education and care settings, the practitioner perspective. *Management in Education*, 28 (4), 156–160. https://doi.org/10.1177/0892020614550467

Department for Education and Skills (DfES) (2005). *Children's Workforce Strategy, Consultation Paper*. London: DfES.

DfES (2006). *Children's Workforce Strategy: Building a World Class Workforce for Children, Young People and Families. The Government Response to the Consultation*. Nottingham: DfES Publications.

Doucet, A. and Mauthner, N. S. (2008). What can be known? Narrated subjects and the Listening Guide. *Qualitative Research*, 8 (3), 399–409.

Dyer, M. A. (2018). *What Does It Mean to Be an Early Years Practitioner: An Investigation into the Professional Identity of Graduate Early Years Practitioners*. Doctoral thesis. University of Huddersfield. http://eprints.hud.ac.uk/id/eprint/34584

Eraut, M. (1994). *Developing Professional Knowledge and Competence*. London: Falmer.

Evetts, J. (2011). A new professionalism? Challenges and opportunities. *Current Sociology*, 59 (4), 406–422.

Foucault, M. (1982). *The subject and power*. In: Dreyfus, H. and Rabinow, P. (eds.), *Michel Foucault: Beyond Structuralism and Hermeneutics*. Chicago: University of Chicago Press.

Hallet, E. (2014). *Leadership of Learning in Early Years Practice*. London: Institute of Education, University of London.

Hargreaves, A. and Fullan, M. (2012). *Professional Capital: Transforming Teaching in Every School*. London: Routledge.

Hordern, J. (2016). Knowledge, practice and the shaping of early years professionalism. *European Early Childhood and Education Research Journal*, 42 (4), 505–520.

Johns, C. (2004). *Becoming a Reflective Practitioner* (2nd ed.). Oxford: Blackwell Publishing.

Lloyd, E. and Hallet, E. (2010). Professionalising the early childhood workforce in England: Work in progress or missed opportunity? *Contemporary Issues in Early Childhood*, 11 (1), 75–88.

Lumsden, E. (2012). *Early Years Professional Status: A new professional or a missed opportunity*. Doctoral Thesis. The University of Northampton.

Mauthner, N. and Doucet, A. (1998). Reflections on a voice-centred relational method: Analyzing maternal and domestic voices. In: Ribbens, J. and Edwards, R. (eds.), *Feminist Dilemmas in Qualitative Research: Public Knowledge and Private Lives*. London: Sage, 119–147.

McDowall Clark, R. and Murray, J. (2012). *Reconceptualising Leadership in the Early Years*. Berkshire: Open University Press.

McMahon, S. (2016). *Early Years Professional Status: A Narrative Study of Leadership and Contradictory Professionalism*. Doctoral Thesis. Sheffield Hallam University. https://ethos.bl.uk/OrderDetails.do?uin=uk.bl.ethos.700580

Oberhuemer, P. (2005). Conceptualising the early childhood pedagogue: Policy approaches and issues of professionalism. *European Early Childhood and Education Research Journal*, 13 (1), 5–16.

Organisation for Economic cooperation and Development OECD (2021). *Starting Strong VI: Supporting Meaningful Interactions in Early Childhood Education and Care*. Starting Strong, OECD Publishing, Paris. https://doi.org/10.1787/f47a06ae-en.

Page, J. (2017). Reframing infant-toddler pedagogy through a lens of professional love: Exploring narratives of professional practice in early childhood settings in England. *Contemporary Issues in Early Childhood*, 18 (4), 387–399.

Page, J. (2018). Characterising the principles of Professional Love in early childhood care and education. *International Journal of Early Years Education*, 26 (2), 125–141.

Rabinow, P. (ed.). (1984). *The Foucault Reader: An Introduction to Foucault's Thought*. London: Penguin.

Sims-Schouten, W. and Strittrich-Lyons, H. (2013). 'Talking the talk': Practical and academic self-concepts of early years practitioners in England. *Journal of Vocational Education and Training*, 66 (1), 39–55.

Siraj, I. and Hallet, E. (2014). *Effective and Caring Leadership in the Early Years*. London: Sage.

Taggart, G. (2011). Don't we care: The ethics and emotional labour of early years professionalism. *Early Years*, 13 (1), 85–95.

Taggart, G. (2014). Compassionate pedagogy: The ethics of care in early childhood professionalism. *European Early Childhood Education Research Journal*, 24 (2), 173–185.

Index

Printed in Great Britain
by Amazon

38121124R00071